DONOR-RESTRICTED GIFTS SIMPLIFIED

by Dan Busby

Dan Busby is a CPA and is Vice President of ECFA. He is a frequent speaker on nonprofit issues in conferences across the U.S. Two of his books have been published annually by Zondervan since 1990: *The Minister's Tax & Financial Guide* and *The Church and Nonprofit Tax & Financial Guide.*

This publication is designed to provide accurate and authoritative information in regard to the subject matter covered. It is distributed with the understanding that the publisher is not engaged in rendering legal, accounting, or other professional service. If legal advice or other expert assistance is required, the services of a competent professional person should be sought.

Every effort has been made to make the materials in this text current as of the date of publication. Federal tax law, however, is subject to change. Congress can modify the law as it has on numerous occasions over the past few years. Also, court decisions and IRS rulings can significantly affect the application of federal tax laws to individual circumstances. Such changes may affect the accuracy of this publication.

ISBN-10: 0-9791914-1-6
ISBN-13: 988-0-9791914-1-1

Acknowledgments

My personal interest in the proper handling of gifts, including donor-restricted gifts, was developed at an early age. The church board of a little church in Lamont, Kansas elected me as the Sunday school treasurer and later as the church treasurer, both while I was still a teenager. I began to understand the importance of properly recording gifts and tracking donor restrictions to ensure the use of those gifts as the donor intended.

Fast-forward ten years or so when I was the founding and managing partner of a CPA firm. There, my opportunities included serving a number of churches and parachurch organizations. It was not uncommon for issues related to donor-restricted gifts to arise during my interaction with clients.

My interest in this topic was particularly heightened when I joined ECFA. It was then I learned how pervasive donor-restricted issues were with the 2,000 organizations served by ECFA.

Many individuals have sharpened my thinking about donor-restricted gifts across the years and I am indebted to each of them. They include: John Butler, Of Counsel, Capin Crouse LLP, Greenwood, IN, Gregg Capin, CPA, Capin Crouse LLP, Atlanta, GA, George R. "Chip" Grange, Attorney, co-founder of Gammon & Grange, Washington, D.C, and Charles "Chip" Watkins, Attorney, Associate with Webster, Chamberlain & Bean, Washington, D.C.

Those who gave of their time and wisdom in reviewing all or a portion of this book and providing many helpful comments included: Gregg Capin, Todd Chasteen, Attorney and CPA, Vice President of Administration, Human Resources and General Counsel, Samaritan's Purse, Boone, NC, Dave Cram, CPA, Corporation Treasurer, Wycliffe International, Orlando, FL, Scott Holbrook, CPA, CFO, Avant Ministries, Kansas City, MO, Richard F. Larkin, CPA, Technical Director, Nonprofit Organizations, BDO Seidman, LLP, Bethesda, MD, Tim Maxwell, CPA, Vice President for Finance, Bible League,

Chicago, IL, and Lloyd Hitoshi Mayer, Associate Professor, Notre Dame Law School, South Bend, IN and Of Counsel, Caplin & Drysdale, Chartered, Washington, D.C.

This book is dedicated to my wife, Claudette, my children, Julie and Alan, and our grandchildren, Daniel and McKenzie. Special thanks goes to my good friend and my first client when I started my CPA firm in Kansas City in 1975, Richard B. Mindlin. He taught me the importance of brevity and communicating key issues. And to my parents, Howard and Bertha Busby: You showed me the way to the Master, taught me the value of integrity and the importance of hard work.

My prayer is that this book will benefit the many churches and other charities who receive donor-restricted gifts, resulting in more funds and funds properly handled. As scriptures tell us: "For we are taking pains to do what is right, not only in the eyes of the Lord but also in the eyes of men" (2 Corinthians 8:21 NIV).

Table of Contents

Introduction

What kind of gift was the largest gift from a single individual to a charity in the history of philanthropy? It was a donor-restricted gift. The gift of $1.5 billion, announced in 2004, was made to The Salvation Army by Mrs. Joan Kroc, widow of McDonalds founder Ray Kroc.

What were the restrictions on the Kroc Gift? It stipulated that half the money go toward the construction of 30 to 50 recreational and educational facilities across the country. The other half of the money was required be put into an endowment whose earnings would pay for operating costs of the facilities, but Mrs. Kroc deliberately did not provide enough to pay for all of the operating costs because she said she wanted The Salvation Army to continue seeking donations from others. Before accepting this gift, the Army had to decide that it could meet the gift restrictions.

Similar to the Kroc gift, many donors take an active interest in the charitable gifts they make to a church or other charity. These gifts can be very effective in funding the charity's projects or other specified causes. The donors have the satisfaction of knowing the gift will accomplish certain of their charitable objectives. A donor-restricted gift can be a win-win situation for both the charity and the donor.

When a charity accepts a contribution that is restricted for a specific purpose, the organization assumes certain fiduciary responsibilities. A fundamental principle for a charity receiving a donor-restricted gift is to honor the donor's restriction(s). Historically, once a gift was complete, most courts held that the donor no longer had standing to enforce the terms of the gift. Those rights now may inure to the public, usually enforceable by the state attorney general's office.

Attorneys general tend to consider their first duty to be the protection of a charity rather than the protection of a donor's wishes. Thus, they have generally sided with the recipient charity, even if its actions seem to conflict with what the donor had in mind. However, recent cases demonstrate that donors and their descendants are applying significant pressure when a charitable gift was used in a manner that was inconsistent with the underlying gift restriction(s) and/or the intention of the donor.[1]

The topic of donor-restricted gifts has been heightened in the public's mind as a result of a high-profile battle between members of the Robertson family against Princeton University.[2] The family of the donor claims the university misused a restricted gift of $35 million that was intended to prepare graduate students for foreign policy careers in the federal government. According to the plaintiffs, only three graduates of the program had gone into public service.

The plaintiffs in the Princeton case authorized a public opinion survey relating to restricted gifts. The survey found that 97 percent of the respondents said they consider it a "very" or "somewhat" serious matter if charities spend donated money for purposes other than as restricted by the donor. Additionally, 78 percent said they would "definitely" or "probably" stop giving to any nonprofit organization that accepts contributions for one purpose and uses the money for another.

Standards established by the Evangelical Council for Financial Accountability (ECFA) are replete with guidance for charities accepting gifts with donor-imposed restrictions:

- All gifts must be under the charity's control (Standard 4).
- Reports must be provided, including financial information, on the specific project for which a charity is soliciting gifts (Standard 5).
- Donor expectations that are created by fund-raising appeals must be realistic and fulfilled through the use of the funds (Standard 7.2).
- Resources must be used and accounted for in accordance with the donor-intended purposes (Standard 7.3).
- Donor-restricted gifts may not be used to pass money or benefits to any named individual for personal use (Standard 7.8).
- Property or gifts-in-kind received by an organization should be acknowledged describing the property or gift accurately without a statement of the gift's market value. It is the responsibility of the

donor to determine the fair market value of the property for tax purposes. The organization may be required to provide additional information for gifts of motor vehicles, boats, and airplanes (Standard 7.10).

- An organization must make every effort to avoid accepting a gift from or entering into a contract with a prospective donor which would knowingly place a hardship on the donor, or place the donor's future well-being in jeopardy (Standard 7.11).

An understanding of the myriad issues discussed in this publication will help a charity navigate the accounting, legal, tax, and integrity topics related to donor-restricted gifts.

Chapter 1

The Basics of Donor-Restricted Gifts

Executive Summary

- The enforcement of a donor's restrictions upon a donee charity is limited to the application of state law.
- A donor-restricted gift is restricted as to time (when a gift may be spent) or purpose (how a gift may be spent) or both.
- Donors may express their gift restrictions explicitly or implicitly.
- While a charity board may designate and undesignate unrestricted net assets, only donors can restrict or unrestrict a gift in terms of time or purpose.
- A gift restriction that is more narrow than the overall purposes of the donee charity is a donor-restricted gift.

Properly handling donor-restricted gifts is a challenge for many charities, secular or religious, church or nonchurch. This is because donor-restricted gifts present a complex combination of accounting, tax, legal, ethical, and other issues.

A donor's written instructions accompanying a gift may provide the basis for a gift restriction. However, in general, a donor's restriction may be either expressed or implied from relevant facts and circumstances.[3] In some instances, the restrictions on donations are driven by the nature of a charity's appeal. For example, if the appeal describes a project, then any response to the appeal is restricted. In other cases, a donor approaches a charity desiring to make a restricted gift. For example, a donor desires to make an endowment gift whereby the gift principal must be held by the charity in perpetuity but the annual earnings may be used for the charity's operations. If the charity accepts the gift with the accompanying restriction, a donor-restricted gift has occurred.[4]

Who may restrict a gift? Only donors can restrict a gift. In an accounting sense, gift restrictions are either temporary or permanent.

Designations of unrestricted assets or net assets by an organization's governing board do not create restrictions. Designations may be reversed by the board and they do not result from a donor's contribution. For example, unrestricted assets or net assets do not become restricted merely because a board designates a portion of them to fund future expenditures for a new building.

Boards can designate (and subsequently un-designate) unrestricted net assets, but boards cannot unrestrict donor-restricted gifts (in limited circumstances, it may be appropriate for a board to use restricted gifts other than for the purpose intended by a donor—see pages 44-48).

In certain situations, donors have the power to unrestrict gifts. For example, a donor restricts a gift for a certain project. Later, the charity asks the donor's permission to redirect the gift for another purpose (unrestricted or restricted) and the donor agrees. The gift is then reclassified from either temporarily or permanently restricted to unrestricted.

Types of restricted contributions. The following are some examples of donor-directed restrictions:

1. **Limitations on gift principal.** Some of the most common donor restrictions on principal include the following:

   a. Spending income earned from the gift principal is permitted but not spending the principal (in accounting terms, this describes a permanently-restricted gift). In the absence of a donor-stipulated provision, if a charity utilizes a spending policy (for example, spending five percent of the fair value of permanently-restricted net assets) and this policy would result in spending gift principal, the donor may need to approve the invasion of principal.

   b. The inflation-adjusted principal of a fund cannot be expended but the appreciation above that amount may be expended.

   c. The principal of a gift may only be expended for specific purposes; *e.g.,* building project, scholarships, benevolence, etc.

   d. Time limitations; *e.g.,* a gift that allows the expenditure of the income earned on the gift principal for five years, after which the principal and income is unrestricted.

   e. Time limitations coupled with any of the three types of restrictions in 1. a, b and c above, on the use of principal; *e.g.,* a gift for a specific purpose with the limitation that the gift must be expended within three years.

2. **Limitations on income earned on gifts until the gift principal is expended.** Donor restrictions on income often fall in the following categories:

   a. **Income accumulation.** Donors may require that income from the gift be accumulated in a variety of ways:

      1) Until a certain time period has elapsed;

      2) Until a certain amount of combined principal and/or income is reached;

3) Until such time as the intended purpose of the accumulation (*e.g.*, construction of a new men's dormitory) needs funding;

4) Accumulation for any other intended purpose.

b. **Restrictions on use of income.** Donors may place a restriction on the use of the income from a gift. These restrictions may be of the same general type as placed upon principal but are often less restrictive. If donors do not restrict the use of income related to a donor-restricted gift, the income generally may be used for unrestricted purposes.

3. **Limitations on investment of a gift.** A donor may place a restriction on how gift funds may be invested (*e.g.*, a gift that could only be invested in securities of the U.S. government).

When charities accept a gift with an understanding that the gift will be invested in a particular manner, the charity's board may be taking on a personal risk. To support the donor's deduction, the charity will need to take the position that it freely decided to make and retain the investment. If the investment performs poorly and was not prudent in light of the overall investments of the charity, the directors could be liable to make up the loss to the charity for an imprudent decision.

When a donor wants a particular investment or desires to have control over investment decisions, it is sometimes possible for the donor to purchase the investment and donate it to the charity or create a limited liability company or partnership that the donor controls and donate a non-managing interest to the charity. In those situations, the board has less exposure because the board did not decide to make the investment and may not be able to change the investment.[5]

The impact of a charity's purpose in determining whether a gift is restricted. The relationship between the charity's purpose(s) and gifts is a fundamental factor in determining whether certain gifts are restricted or unrestricted. If a gift purpose is not more specific than the broad limits imposed by the charity's purpose and nature, the gift is generally unrestricted. However, if a gift purpose is more specific than the broad limits imposed by the charity's purpose and nature, the gift is restricted.

The Impact of a Charity's Purpose on Gifts

Unrestricted gift	Restricted gift
▪ Gift is for a purpose that is not more specific than the broad limits imposed by the charity's purpose and nature	▪ Gift is for a purpose more specific than the broad limits imposed by the charity's purpose and nature, such as: ➢ Restricted for a country ➢ Restricted for a project ➢ Other time or purpose restrictions

Often a gift comes in as the result of a fund-raising appeal. The appeal's wording may affect whether or not the gift is restricted as reflected in the following examples.

<table>
<tr><td colspan="2">Example #1
Fund-raising appeal matches the broad limits imposed by the charity's general purpose and nature.</td></tr>
<tr><td>Charity Purpose(s)</td><td>To uphold the sanctity of human life by ministering to women and families in our community who are facing unexpected pregnancies</td></tr>
<tr><td>Fund-raising Appeals</td><td>The fund-raising appeals only reference the charity's general purpose and nature.</td></tr>
<tr><td>Accounting Treatment</td><td>Since the fund-raising appeals match (e.g., are not more narrow than) the broad purpose of the charity, gifts in response to these fund-raising appeals are unrestricted revenue.</td></tr>
</table>

<table>
<tr><td colspan="4">Example #2
Certain fund-raising appeals match the charity's general purpose and nature and some appeals are more specific than the charity's general purpose and nature.</td></tr>
<tr><td>Charity Purpose(s)</td><td colspan="3">To uphold the sanctity of human life by ministering to women and families in our community who are facing unexpected pregnancies</td></tr>
<tr><td>Fund-raising Appeals</td><td>Certain fund-raising appeals only reference the charity's general purpose(s).</td><td>For teen pregnancy educational programs</td><td>For new equipment for the office</td></tr>
<tr><td>Accounting Treatment</td><td>Since the fund-raising appeals match (e.g., are not more specific than) the general purpose and nature of the charity, gifts in response to these fund-raising appeals are unrestricted revenue.</td><td colspan="2">Since both of these appeals are more specific than the charity's general purpose and nature, all gifts received in response to these appeals are temporarily restricted. (Note: Since these appeals do not request funds for projects that might be permanently restricted [e.g., endowment], the donor restrictions are only temporary.)</td></tr>
</table>

Discretion and control—If the charity notifies the donors that the charity will exercise discretion and control over the gifts for the educational program and the equipment, this fact does not change the temporarily-restricted nature of the gifts. (See pages 14-20 for additional discussion of this topic.)

Example #3

Certain fund-raising appeals match the charity's general purpose and nature and some appeals are more specific than the charity's general purpose and nature.

Charity Purpose(s)	To evangelize the nations for Christ through evangelism and church planting teams, theological and leadership training, and outreach through medical clinics and radio stations			
Fund-raising Appeals	Certain fund-raising appeals only reference the charity's general purpose(s).	For medical clinics	For leadership training (seminaries)	For evangelism and church planting
Accounting Treatment	Since the fund-raising appeals match (*e.g.*, are not more specific than the general purpose and nature of the charity), gifts in response to these fund-raising appeals are unrestricted revenue.	Since both of these appeals are more specific than the charity's general purpose and nature, all gifts received in response to these appeals are temporarily restricted. (Note: Since these appeals do not request funds for projects that might be permanently restricted [*e.g.*, endowment], the donor restrictions are only temporary.)		Since evangelism and church planting purposes are components of the charity's general purpose and nature, all gifts received in response to these appeals are temporarily restricted. (*Note:* Since these appeals do not request funds for projects that might be permanently restricted [*e.g.*, endowment], the donor restrictions are only temporary.) Even if evangelism and church planting had been the only purposes of this charity, the charity may expand its activities in the future and yet the use of the funds received in response to this appeal should still be restricted to evangelism and church planting.

Discretion and control—If the charity notifies the donors that the charity will exercise discretion and control over the gifts for the medical clinics, and leadership training, this fact does not change the temporarily-restricted nature of the gifts. (See pages 14-20 for additional discussion of this topic.)

Example #4

Certain fund-raising appeals match the charity's general purpose and nature and some appeals are more specific than the charity's general purpose and nature.

<table>
<tr><td>Charity Purpose(s)</td><td colspan="9">To provide scriptures and training worldwide so that individuals will be brought into the fellowship of Christ and His church</td></tr>
<tr><td rowspan="2">Fund-raising Appeals</td><td rowspan="2">Certain fund-raising appeals only reference the charity's general purpose(s).</td><td colspan="8">Scriptures and training for
Country</td></tr>
<tr><td>A</td><td>B</td><td>C</td><td>D</td><td>E</td><td>F</td><td>G</td><td>H</td></tr>
<tr><td>Accounting Treatment</td><td>Since the fund-raising appeals match (e.g., are not more specific than the general purpose and nature of the charity), gifts in response to these fund-raising appeals are unrestricted revenue.</td><td colspan="8">Since these appeals for Scriptures and training for certain countries are location-specific, this constitutes a temporarily-restricted project. (Note: Since these appeals do not request funds for projects that might be permanently restricted [e.g., endowment], the donor restrictions are only temporary.)</td></tr>
</table>

Discretion and control—If the charity notifies the donors that the charity will exercise discretion and control over the gifts for Scriptures and training, including for certain countries, this fact does not change the temporarily-restricted nature of the gifts. (See pages 14-20 for additional discussion of this topic.)

Chapter Review 1

1. If a charity does not spend a donor-restricted gift within the limits of a donor's restriction, can a donor obtain relief in the federal court system? Generally, no. Enforcement of donor-restrictions is generally a state law issue.

2. To restrict a gift, is a donor required to provide a written restriction with a gift? This is one way for a donor to restrict a gift but certainly not the only way. A donor's restrictions may be either expressed or implied from relevant facts and circumstances. In most instances, restrictions are driven by the nature of the charity's appeal.

3. When a donor restricts a gift, how is the gift classified for accounting purposes? As either temporarily or permanently restricted.

4. May charities restrict gifts? No—only donors may restrict gifts. Additionally, only a donor may generally remove or change the restriction placed by the donor on a particular gift.

5. May charities designate an organization's net assets? Yes, a charity's board may designate unrestricted net assets (and subsequently lift the designation). Care must be exercised to only designate unrestricted net assets that qualify for designation. For example, unrestricted net assets includes a charity's property, plant and equipment, net of related debt. This amount is not available for designation.

6. Can a charity's purpose impact the determination of whether a gift is donor-restricted? Yes. If the purpose of the gift is more specific than the general purpose and nature of the charity, the gift is restricted (either temporarily or permanently). For example, if the charity's purpose and nature is to feed children, a gift to build a new administrative office for the charity is more specific than the general purpose and nature of the charity. Therefore, the gift is donor restricted.

Chapter 2

Charity Control, Donor Control, and Donor Preferences

Executive Summary

- Boards must exercise overall discretion and control over a charity's resources. This is fundamental to ensure that a charity's resources are used for tax-exempt purposes.
- When a donor restricts a donation, the gift is just a portion of the charity's overall resources under the control of the charity's board. The board may exercise overall control while honoring the donor's restrictions. Therefore, board control and donor restrictions are complementary.
- A donor's preference, in connection with a gift, expresses a desire or suggestion which is advisory in nature. The preference does not restrict the use of the gift as to time or purpose. A preference allows the charity's full discretion to use the gift in relation to the donor's desire or suggestion or to use the funds for any other purpose.
- It may be inappropriate for a charity to accept a gift if the gift restrictions:
  - prevent the charity from using the donation in the furtherance of its charitable purposes,
  - are incompatible with the charity's general purpose and nature,
  - mandate that the funds be used in part for the benefit of the donor or the donor's relatives, or
  - are at odds with the best interests of the charity.

A common misconception is that the discretion and control a charity board must exercise over any gift is in conflict with, or contradictory to, donor restrictions on a gift. *This is not true.* Some believe that organizations should not follow donor restrictions, from time to time, to demonstrate their control. *This is inappropriate.*

Board control and donor restrictions are complementary. It is not *either/or* but *both/and*! Restricted gifts must be used for a specific exempt purpose, whereas unrestricted gifts may be used for any exempt purpose.

It may be inappropriate for a charity to accept a gift under some gift restrictions.

- **A gift should not prevent the charity from using the donation in the furtherance of its charitable purposes.** For example, if a donor restricts a gift for the benefit of a specific individual in a way that prevents the charity from exercising discretion and control over the gift (such as a gift restricted for a particular benevolent recipient, an employee of the charity, etc.), the gift is generally not deductible as a charitable contribution (see Chapter 5 for additional discussion of this topic).

- **Restrictions should not be incompatible with the mission of the charity.** Even though a restricted gift is exclusively charitable, it would be inappropriate for a charity to accept a gift requiring the expenditure of funds outside the mission of the charity. For example, if a ministry whose sole purpose is international child sponsorship is offered a gift restricted for inner-city evangelism in the U.S., the gift should not be accepted by the charity because it is inconsistent with the mission of the charity (the overall mission of the charity is generally described in the organization's governing documents).

- **Restrictions should not mandate that the funds be used for the benefit of the donor or the donor's relatives.** By requiring that a gift be used to benefit the donor's relatives, the restriction results in the gift being used for noncharitable purposes, and therefore does not qualify as a charitable contribution.[6]

- **Restrictions should not be at odds with the best interests of the charity.** A restricted gift could be exclusively charitable and compatible with the mission of the charity and still not be in the best interests of the charity. A charity might not have the capacity to comply with gift restrictions. For example, the amount of funds raised for a particular disaster may exceed the charity's capacity to effectively spend the funds in a reasonable period of time.

The administrative requirements of a restricted gift could consume an inordinate amount of the charity's resources.

Example 1: Even a gift of "fee simple" residential property can result in substantial costs and be very difficult for a charity to sell.

Example 2: The gift of a time share property could be offered to a ministry. However, the charity may decide the time share is not in the best interest of the charity because (1) time shares are often unmarketable properties laden with annual costs, and (2) even when sales are made, the low resale market prices can minimize or erase profits.

Special care should often be exercised with respect to non-cash gifts. For example, a charity should generally refuse a noncash restricted gift if:

- the time and costs of handling the asset are disproportionate to its expected value,
- the charity's exposure to liability is excessive, or
- the charity's prospects of receiving cash are distant and disproportionate to the current costs of holding the asset.

The nature of a donor-restricted gift does not change from temporarily restricted to unrestricted because discretion and control is exercised by the charity over the gift.

Example: A donor restricts a gift to a charity by responding to a solicitation for a certain project, or a donor checks a "Building Fund" box on an offering envelope at a church.

A charity's policy of not accepting donor-restricted gifts (see pages 129-30) nor using disclaimers (see pages 48-51) such as "Our organization provides discretion and control over all gifts" or "All gifts are considered unrestricted" do not change the nature of the gift from temporarily restricted to unrestricted.

In this example, the gift should be used in accordance with the donor's restriction, the donor should be asked if the charity may redirect the gift for another use (restricted or unrestricted), or the gift should be returned to the donor.

Discretion and control. The board must exercise discretion and control over all contributions to an exempt organization to be used exclusively for its exempt purposes, unrestricted and restricted. In addition, the board must provide reasonable measures to assure that donor-restricted gifts are used for the intended exempt purpose(s). Donor-preferenced gifts may require the highest level of due diligence by a charity to ensure the preference does not constitute a gift earmarked for an individual (see page 15).

There are three levels of discretion and control that an organization may be required to provide with respect to nonprofit resources. Distinguishing between these three levels is fundamental.

- **Level 1: Discretion and control over *all* nonprofit resources.** Charities must exercise a broad level of discretion and control with respect to the use of all charity resources (gifts, fees, sales, investment income, etc.). This includes assurance that funds are expended within the charitable purposes of the organization and that funds are not used for private inurement, private benefit, and excess benefit transactions.

- **Level 2: Discretion and control over donor-restricted gifts that are not donor-preferenced for an individual.** Donor-restricted gifts require a higher level of discretion and control than in Level 1 for all nonprofit resources but lower than for donor-preferenced gifts in Level 3. In addition to the broad discretion and control described in Level 1, the charity must determine if the donor restrictions are compatible with the charity's mission and are in the best interest of the charity.

- **Level 3: Discretion and control exercised over donor-restricted gifts that are also donor-preferenced for an individual.** Donor-preferenced gifts require the highest discretion and control when gifts are preferenced by a donor to support the work of a particular individual or to provide support for a particular benevolent recipient.

Notifying the donor on the gift response form that the charity will exercise control and discretion over the gift does not remove the organization's responsibility to honor the donor's restriction placed on a gift (see pages 6-8). Charities must exercise control and discretion over all charitable gifts, whether unrestricted (may be used for any exempt purpose) or restricted (must be used for a specific purpose) by the donor.

Donor preferences contrasted to donor restrictions. In charitable giving, there is a distinction between a donor's restriction and a donor's preference. This distinction can make a difference between the donor's eligibility for a charitable tax deduction and no tax deduction.

Although some donor-preferenced gifts are for a specified purpose or project and, therefore, are temporarily restricted, the preferencing of a gift does not dictate whether the gift is unrestricted or restricted. When a gift is preferenced to support a particular worker, the gift may qualify for a charitable tax deduction.[7] However, other factors must be reviewed to determine whether the gift is unrestricted or restricted for accounting purposes.

> ***Example 1:*** Accompanying a gift, a donor communicates to the charity: "My preference is that the gift be used for scholarships. However, I give the charity permission to use the gift for any purpose consistent with the charity's mission statement." This gift is an unrestricted gift because the charity has full discretion as to the use of the gift.

> ***Example 2:*** A prayer letter or appeal letter from a charity that conducts work in *several countries* describes the need for religious workers in India. The request is for funds to enable a particular worker employed by the

charity to carry out certain activity in India. A gift in response to this appeal is temporarily restricted because (1) the gift is for a specific activity and (2) the gift is for the ministry's program in India and the charity conducts work in several countries, *i.e.,* there is a specific activity and geographic restriction. The preferencing of the gift to support a particular worker generally does not impact the determination of whether the gift is unrestricted or temporarily restricted.

A donor's *restriction,* in connection with a gift, limits the charity's use of the funds to the purposes specified by the donor, *e.g.,* "This gift is made on the condition that," or "This gift is restricted for XYZ project." This type of gift is generally tax-deductible as a charitable contribution.

A donor's *preference,* in connection with a gift, expresses a desire, suggestion, or interest which is advisory in nature. The preference does not restrict the use of the gift as to time or to purpose. The preference allows the charity's full discretion to use the gift in relation to the donor's desire or suggestion or to use the funds for any other purpose. Factors that imply a charity has received a donor-preferenced gift and not a restricted gift include the following:

- The donor intends only to express a desire or make a suggestion with respect to a gift.

- Both the solicitation letter and response form (and perhaps the gift acknowledgment) from the charity clearly communicate to the donor that preferenced gifts are sought.

- The donor communicated in writing or verbally a desire or suggestion as to the use of the funds, but the donor did not restrict the funds to a certain purpose.

Example 1: A charity's solicitation materials describe a capital campaign which includes several components (a building, funding for a certain ministry program, and endowment funds). The communication clarifies that funds are sought for the campaign as a whole. However, the solicitation states that donors may indicate a preference for one or more campaign components (building, program, or endowment). The appeal also states that while the charity will try to honor such donor preferences, the charity will exercise appropriate discretion and control over all campaign gifts.

Option A: A donor contributes $5,000 and does not indicate a preference for one of the campaign components. The charity acknowledges the gift as a contribution to the overall campaign and uses its discretion in applying the gift to campaign purposes.

Option B: A donor contributes $5,000 and indicates a preference that the gift be used for the building component of the campaign. The charity, while acknowledging the donor's preference, states they will use their discretion and control in utilizing the gift for campaign purposes.

In both Options A and B, the charity has properly communicated (in the appeal and the gift acknowledgment) to the donor.

Example 2: A charity's solicitation materials describe a project to build, staff and develop a missions training center in Mexico. The response form is consistent with the appeal language, giving donors an opportunity to check a box indicating a gift for the missions training center. The following disclaimer statement was included at the bottom of the response form: "All gifts are under the discretion and control of the charity."

Option A: The charity appropriately records the gifts raised in response to this appeal as temporarily-restricted revenue, expends the funds for the missions training center, and fulfills the donor's restrictions.

Option B: The charity does not properly account for the funds raised in response to this appeal.

> Instead, the charity inappropriately records the gifts as unrestricted and uses the gifts to help fund the charity's annual budget. The charity's treatment of the gifts is based on its position that the "discretion and control" disclaimer statement on the response form changes what would have been temporarily-restricted gifts to donor-preferenced gifts, eligible for unrestricted treatment.
>
> These gifts should be recorded as temporarily-restricted revenue. The discretion and control on the response form is appropriate (but not necessary). The charity should have discretion and control over these gifts to ensure they are used for the missions training center in Mexico whether a "discretion and control" disclaimer statement is communicated to donors or not.

In limited situations, it may be appropriate for a charity to redirect restricted gifts for purposes other than intended by the donor. The redirection should be based on an explicit contingency policy that is clearly communicated to the donor. For example, a charity raises gifts for a specific project. The solicitation explains the charity's policy of redirecting any gifts received in excess of project needs for similar projects conducted by the charity. If the excess amount redirected is insignificant, the redirection is generally appropriate.

It is inconsistent to treat gifts as only preferenced based on internal policy if the solicitation literature and donor expectations indicate gifts will be restricted for specified purposes. Treating a donor-restricted gift as only donor preferenced is an inappropriate and ineffective attempt by a charity to remove donor restrictions.

If the donor preferences a gift, even when the preference is for the funds to go to a particular individual, the gift may qualify for a charitable tax deduction if the charity exercises adequate control with respect to the gift. For example, a gift restricted for missions and preferenced for missionary endeavors involving a certain identified individual (see pages 79-81 for gifts under the deputized fund-raising concept) or a gift for benevolence preferenced for a particular benevolent recipient (see pages 62-63) may qualify for a charitable tax deduction if the charity exercises adequate control related to the gift.

Example: A charity has a benevolence fund and a donor offers to make a $500 gift to the fund and indicates a preference that the gift be used to assist a particular needy family.

Option A: The donor's intent is to make a charitable gift to and for the charity; it is not the donor's intent to make a gift to the needy family. The donor's preference that the gift be used for the particular family is secondary to the donor's intent to make a gift to and for the charity.

The charity provides the donor with a gift receipt, subjects the gift to the charity's benevolence fund policies and procedures, and decides to distribute the $500 to the needy family for which the gift was preferenced.

The fact that the charity distributed the exact amount of the gift to the family preferenced by the donor does not generally negate the charitable gift since the charity's benevolence fund policies and procedures were appropriately applied.

Option B: The donor's intent is the same as in Option A. The charity provides the donor with a gift receipt, subjects the gift to the charity's benevolence fund policies and procedures, and uses the $500 for benevolent recipients other than the family for which the gift was preferenced.

The charity has appropriately exercised discretion and control over the gift. While considering the donor preference to assist a particular family, the charity determined that the funds should go to other benevolent recipients.

Option C: Although the donor says it is only his preference that the gift go to a certain needy family, through other statements it is clear the donor's intent is to make a gift to and for a particular needy family, not to benefit the charity.

Since this appears to be a gift earmarked for certain individuals, the charity should not accept the gift. The acceptance of an earmarked gift is not consistent with a charity's tax-exempt purpose.

Should a donor place the name of a preferenced worker on the memo line of the donor's check? If the donor writes "to Joe Smith" or "for Joe Smith," it could suggest the gift is earmarked and endanger the charitable deduction. It is generally advisable for the donor to simply check a box on a response form indicating a preference to support the ministry of a particular worker. This presumes the response form is properly worded ("preferenced for the ministry of Joe Smith"), and not improperly worded ("for Joe Smith").

Donor-advised gifts. Donor-advised gifts may be made to a donor-advised fund (DAF).[8] Although DAFs have been used for many years, the concept was only codified in 2006.[9] A DAF is defined as a fund or account that is separately identified by reference to contributions of a donor or donors, is owned and controlled by a charitable sponsoring organization, and to which a donor (or any person appointed or designated by the donor) has advisory privileges with respect to the distribution or investment of amounts in the fund. The right of a donor to make recommendations to the trustees of a DAF generally does not constitute a restricted gift.

Example: A donor makes an irrevocable contribution of cash and/or securities to the separate DAF or account. The donor is eligible for a tax deduction at the time of the contribution to the DAF even though the DAF may distribute the funds to one or more charities in a subsequent tax year. Subsequent to the date of the gift, the donor makes recommendations to the trustees for grants to be made out of his or her

> separate fund. To decide whether to approve or deny the grants, the representatives of the sponsoring organization review the recommended grants to verify whether the potential recipient organization is a qualified charity and whether other appropriate criteria are met.

A DAF is responsible to provide gift acknowledgments to its donors. When a DAF distributes funds to a charity, the recipient charity should not provide a gift receipt to the taxpayer who made the donation. However, it is appropriate for the charity to express appreciation, other than by a formal gift acknowledgment.

Chapter Review 2

1. Is a charity responsible to exercise discretion and control over all its resources? Yes. Charities must exercise a broad level of discretion and control with respect to the use of all charity resources (gifts, fees, sales, investment income, etc.).

2. Is the exercise of overall discretion and control (see question #1) in conflict with a donor's restrictions on a gift? No. Exercising overall discretion and control and following the restrictions of a donor are complementary concepts.

3. How does a donor preference differ from a donor restriction? A donor preference does not restrict the use of a gift—it is only a desire or suggestion which is advisory in nature. A donor restriction limits the charity's use of the funds to the purposes specified by the donor.

4. If a charity precisely complies with a donor's preference with respect to a gift, does this disqualify the gift for charitable deduction purposes? Not necessarily. Key factors include the donor's intent to make a gift to the charity and the extent to which the charity applies discretion and control over the gift.

5. Is it ever inappropriate for a charity to accept a donor-restricted gift? Yes. Gifts should not be accepted if they are incompatible with the charity's mission and/or are not in the best interests of the charity.

6. When a charity receives a distribution from a donor-advised fund (DAF), does the charity provide a gift acknowledgment to the donor who made the donation to the DAF? No. The donor receives a gift acknowledgment directly from the DAF.

Chapter 3

Charity Communications and Donor Responses

Executive Summary

- A donor must intend to benefit a charity for a gift to qualify for charitable deduction purposes.
- A donor may restrict a donation explicitly or implicitly. Charities must honor both types of restrictions if it accepts the gift.
- There must be consistency in a charity's fund-raising appeal, its response form and all other communications related to the appeal. Such consistency is fundamental to the donor's clear understanding of the charity's appeal.
- Challenge gifts are not dependent upon gifts by other donors.
- Matching gifts are conditional on gifts being made by other donors, either unrestricted or restricted, either with or without a time limit.
- Special care is required to adequately communicate the anticipated use of gifts when a capital campaign or another appeal has multiple components. This is particularly important when campaign goals are not achieved.
- When the word "endowment" is used by itself, it generally refers to the permanent restriction of a gift. However, the general meaning of the word endowment may change when the words "term" or "quasi" are used with it. A term endowment is a temporary restriction of a gift—restricted for a term of time. A quasi-endowment is an unrestricted endowment that functions like a permanent endowment.

To qualify for a charitable deduction, a donor must have a charitable intent with respect to a payment to a charity.[10] While this sounds subjective, the IRS and the courts do not rely on secrets in the donor's heart. They examine communication from the charity to the donor and by the donor to the charity.

All statements made by the organization in its fund-raising appeals about the use of the gift must be honored by the organization (ECFA Standard 7.3). Charities must also honor implicit donor restrictions, even going above and beyond what the law may require, to do what integrity requires.

A donor's intent or direction may be expressed in the following ways:

- **Explicitly.** In many cases, donor restrictions are explicit. A donor may send a letter specifying that the contribution be used for a certain program (or restricted for a future period of time). Or a charity distributes a letter or a newsletter (it could be an explicit fund-raising letter or it may be a "prayer letter") and includes a response form with the letter. The donor indicates a restriction on the response form: by checking a box corresponding to a restricted gift option, by indicating the restriction on the response form, by indicating the restriction on a check or in a separate written communication accompanying the gift.

- **Implicitly.** Donor restrictions can be implied if the circumstances surrounding the contribution make clear the donor's intended restriction on the use of the assets.[11] For example, a donor makes a gift in response to a solicitation which requests funds for a particular project. Although the donor may not have explicitly communicated the restriction with the gift, the stated objective of the fund-raising appeal makes the donor's restriction clear.[12]

The impact of charity appeals and donor's responses to them. Charity appeals and donor responses must be considered as a whole. The donor's intent is related to both what was communicated in the appeal and to any donor instructions accompanying the gift. Focusing solely on the solicitation or the donor's instructions may not be sufficient. Inconsistencies or ambiguities in one or the other may cause uncertainty.

A charity should ensure consistency in the fund-raising appeals, the response form and all other communications related to an appeal. If, for example, certain needs are communicated in the appeal which could give rise to a temporarily-restricted gift, a response form should communicate the same fund-raising needs. A response form may also provide giving opportunities unrelated to the appeal such as an opportunity to give "where needed most." (See examples of fund-raising appeals on pages 6-8.)

A charity is obligated to use a donation as directed by the donor or, alternatively, to return the donation. Once the donor has indicated the intent for the donation and the charity has accepted the gift, it is the responsibility of the charity to fulfill that intent.

Donor intent is normally determined in one of two ways:

- **The donor responds to a specific appeal.** If the appeal is more specific than the broad limits imposed by the charity's purpose and nature, the appeal should clearly identify the purpose for which donations are sought. If the donor simply responds to the appeal, it is reasonable to assume that the donor's intent is that the funds be used as described in the appeal. This highlights the need for precise communication in the appeal in order to establish a clear understanding between the charity and the donor about how the donation will be used.

- **The donor communicates specific intent, written or verbal, to a charity.** Specific donor restrictions may be communicated in letters accompanying a gift, notes on the gift response piece, or personal conversations with the donor. Any communication accompanying the gift should be considered an expression of donor intent.

To state the principle in the negative: the charity should not use gifts for purposes other than those intended by the donor.

Example 1: An appeal letter is very general in nature presenting only the overall needs of the charity and also describes some of the current program activities. The donor sends a gift with the response form that accompanied the request for general funds. However, the donor notes on the response form that he or she wants the gift to be used for computer equipment. This is a temporarily-restricted gift.

Example 2: An appeal letter is very specific in presenting a need for funds for a building project. However, the donor checks the box "use where needed most." This is an unrestricted gift.

Example 3: Same specific appeal letter as Example 2. The donor sends a check with the response form, but does not check any of the boxes on the form and there is not a restrictive notation on the memo line of the check. This is a restricted gift by implication since it was generated by a specific request and the donor was silent as to the specificity of the gift.

Example 4: Same specific appeal letter as Example 2. The donor sends a check but does not include the response form in the envelope and does not place a restrictive notation on the memo line of the check. If the check is inserted in an envelope provided by the charity and it is possible to identify the particular appeal for the building fund based on the envelope (for example, the envelope has "Building Fund" imprinted on it), this gift is implicitly restricted for the building fund.

The examples on page 27-32 illustrate several fundamental principles relating to appeals, response forms relating to the appeals, and the proper accounting treatment of the gifts:

- **The appeal in relation to the charity's mission.** A charity should review an appeal to determine if the appeal is more specific than the broad limits imposed by the charity's purpose and nature. If so, the gifts resulting from the appeal are generally temporarily restricted.
- **The consistency of an appeal and the response form.** When drafting a solicitation, a charity should consider a particular appeal and response form as a whole. Consistency between the appeal and the response form is fundamental. If the appeal letter describes a certain project, the response form should provide an opportunity to give to that same project.

<table>
<tr><th colspan="3">Appeal Letter #1</th></tr>
<tr><td>Appeal</td><td colspan="2">An appeal letter solicits contributions for a church building project in Indonesia</td></tr>
<tr><td>Response Form</td><td colspan="2">☐ I/We praise God with you for the way He has worked in Indonesia and in so many other places over the past year! I/We want to make sure that these efforts can continue to move full speed ahead, unhindered by lack of funding for the construction of a church in Bantul, Indonesia. Enclosed is a gift of:
☐ $50 ☐ $100 ☐ $250 ☐ $500 ☐ $1,000 ☐ $________
☐ $_______ Please use where needed most.
Make checks payable to: ABC Charity
Mr. and Mrs. John Smith
1234 Main Street, #123
Orlando, FL 32832-1000</td></tr>
<tr><td>Accounting Treatment</td><td>This is a temporarily-restricted gift if the donor responded to the appeal letter and:
• checked the first box or
• didn't check any box or
• didn't use the response form.
Note: In these last two options, the gift is temporarily restricted for the church construction if it is apparent to the charity that the gift is in response to the appeal, whether or not the donor checked the first box or didn't even use the response form—the use of a certain envelope might indicate a gift relates to this appeal.</td><td>This is an unrestricted gift if the donor:
• checked the "where needed most" box or
• wrote "unrestricted gift" or similar wording on the memo line of the check or
• left the memo line blank on the check but enclosed a memo, letter, or other writing instructing that the gift may be used for unrestricted purposes.</td></tr>
</table>

<table>
<tr><th colspan="3">Appeal Letter #2</th></tr>
<tr><td>Appeal</td><td colspan="2">An appeal letter solicits contributions for a capital campaign. The appeal envisions temporarily-restricted gifts since no needs are described which would give rise to a permanently-restricted gift; i.e., the appeal did not include an endowment component.</td></tr>
<tr><td>Response Form

The response vehicle is general and does not mention the capital campaign.</td><td colspan="2">☐ I/We praise God with you for the way He has worked in the ministry! I/We want to make sure that these efforts can continue to move full speed ahead, unhindered by lack of funding for the basic building blocks of ministry. Enclosed is a gift of:

☐ $50 ☐ $100 ☐ $250 ☐ $500 ☐ $1,000 ☐ $________

Make checks payable to: ABC Charity

Mr. and Mrs. John Smith
1234 Main Street, #123
Orlando, FL 32832-1000</td></tr>
<tr><td>Accounting Treatment</td><td>This is a temporarily-restricted gift for the capital campaign whether a donor:
• enclosed the response form or
• did not enclose the response form.

Note: In these two options, the gift is temporarily-restricted for the capital campaign if it is apparent to the charity that the gift is in response to the appeal, whether or not the donor checked the first box or didn't even use the response form—the use of a certain envelope might indicate a gift relates to this appeal.</td><td>This is an unrestricted gift if the donor:
• wrote "unrestricted gift" or similar wording on the memo line of the check or
• left the memo line blank on the check but enclosed a memo, letter, or other writing instructing that the gift is for unrestricted purposes.</td></tr>
</table>

<table>
<tr><th colspan="3">Appeal Letter #3</th></tr>
<tr><td>Appeal</td><td colspan="2">An appeal letter describes two needs: an orphanage in India and drilling water wells in Nigeria</td></tr>
<tr><td>Response Form
This is an inappropriately designed response vehicle because it only mentions the orphanage, not the water wells.</td><td colspan="2">☐ I/We praise God with you for the way He has worked in India and in so many other places over the past year! I/We want to make sure that these efforts can continue to move full speed ahead, unhindered by lack of funding for the orphanage in India. Enclosed is a gift of:
☐ $50 ☐ $100 ☐ $250 ☐ $500 ☐ $1,000 ☐ $________
☐ $_______ Please use where needed most.
Make checks payable to: ABC Charity
Mr. and Mrs. John Smith
1234 Main Street, #123
Orlando, FL 32832-1000</td></tr>
<tr><td>Accounting Treatment</td><td>This is a temporarily-restricted gift that must be allocated by the charity between the orphanage and the drilling of water wells projects if a donor:
• did not check the “where needed most” box or
• did not use the response form.
Note: In these two options, the gift is temporarily restricted for the two needs referenced in the appeal, whether or not the donor checked the first box or didn’t even use the response form—the use of a certain envelope might indicate a gift relates to this appeal. In this case the appeal wording overrides the response form.</td><td>This is an unrestricted gift if the donor:
• checked the “where needed most” box or
• wrote “unrestricted gift” or similar wording on the memo line of the check or
• left the memo line blank on the check but enclosed a memo, letter, or other writing instructing that the gift is for unrestricted purposes.</td></tr>
</table>

<table>
<tr><th colspan="3">Appeal Letter #4</th></tr>
<tr><td>Appeal</td><td colspan="2">An appeal letter describes the need to build the charity's endowment fund</td></tr>
<tr><td>Response Form

The response vehicle properly references the endowment fund, corresponding to the appeal.</td><td colspan="2">☐ I/We praise God with you for the way He has worked in the ministry over the past year! I/We want to make sure that these efforts can continue to move full speed ahead, unhindered by lack of funding for endowment purposes. Enclosed is a gift of:

☐ $50 ☐ $100 ☐ $250 ☐ $500 ☐ $1,000 ☐ $________
☐ $_______ Please use where needed most.
Make checks payable to: ABC Charity

Mr. and Mrs. John Smith
1234 Main Street, #123
Orlando, FL 32832-1000</td></tr>
<tr><td>Accounting Treatment</td><td>This is a permanently-restricted gift if a donor:
• checked the first box or
• did not check any box or
• did not use the response form.

Note: In these three options, the gift is permanently restricted for the endowment fund, whether or not the donor checked the first box or didn't even use the response form—the use of a certain envelope might indicate a gift related to this appeal. The term "endowment" generally implies a permanently-restricted gift instead of an unrestricted or temporarily-restricted gift.</td><td>This is an unrestricted gift if a donor:
• checked the "where needed most" box or
• wrote "unrestricted gift" or similar wording on the memo line of the check or
• left the memo line blank on the check but enclosed a memo, letter, or other writing instructing that the gift may be used for unrestricted purposes.</td></tr>
</table>

Appeal Letter #5

Appeal

An appeal letter describes the following capital campaign:

$6 million to construct a certain building
$3 million for scholarships (not endowed)
$1 million for the operating fund

Responses needs will generate both temporarily-restricted gifts for the first two *and* unrestricted funds for the last.

Response Form

The response vehicle properly references the capital campaign, corresponding to the appeal.

☐ I/We praise God with you for the way He has worked in the ministry over the past year! I/We want to make sure that these efforts can continue to move full speed ahead, unhindered by lack of funding for the capital campaign needs. Enclosed is a gift of:

☐ $50 ☐ $100 ☐ $250 ☐ $500 ☐ $1,000 ☐ $________

Make checks payable to: ***ABC Charity***

Mr. and Mrs. John Smith
1234 Main Street, #123
Orlando, FL 32832-1000

Accounting Treatment

Gifts received for the capital campaign in response to this appeal will include both temporarily-restricted and unrestricted funds.

The following are two possible scenarios:

1. **The capital campaign goal is achieved.** Gifts of $10 million are received. The gifts should be allocated based on the campaign components as follows unless the charity has clearly communicated to donors that a different allocation of funds will occur:

	Appeal	Appeal %	Actual
Building	$6 million	60%	$6 million
Scholarships	3 million	30	3 million
Unrestricted	1 million	10	1 million

2. **The capital campaign goal is not achieved.** Gifts of $9 million are received in contrast to the $10 million goal. The $9 million of gifts should be allocated based on the campaign components as follows unless the charity has clearly communicated to donors that a different allocation of funds will occur:

	Appeal	Appeal %	Actual
Building	$6 million	60%	$5.4 million
Scholarships	3 million	30	2.7 million
Unrestricted	1 million	10	.9 million

Appeal Letter #6

Appeal	An appeal letter describes the following capital campaign: $6 million to construct a fine arts building $3 million for scholarships $1 million for the operating fund Responses to the first two needs will generate temporarily-restricted gifts and the last need is for unrestricted funds.
Response Form The response vehicle properly references the capital campaign, corresponding to the appeal.	☐ Please use my gift for the campaign as indicated: $__________ Fine Arts building construction $__________ Scholarships $__________ Operating fund $__________ For the capital campaign in general *Make checks payable to:* ***ABC Charity*** Mr. and Mrs. John Smith 1234 Main Street, #123 Orlando, FL 32832-1000
Accounting Treatment Gifts received for the capital campaign in response to this appeal will include both temporarily-restricted and unrestricted funds.	Donors were permitted to either give to the capital campaign as a whole or to identify certain components of the campaign as restricted purposes of their gifts. The scholarship component was fully funded by gifts restricted specifically for that purpose. The gifts given to the campaign as a whole may be allocated between the other two campaign components only if the charity clearly communicates the allocation of the funds, either before or after the donations are made. *Note:* This example emphasizes the need to appropriately plan for potential overfunding of a campaign component before any funds are raised.

- Accounting treatment in relation to the appeal and the response form. The accounting treatment has a relation to the appeal and the response form, taken as a whole. Communication to a donor in the appeal may have a bearing on the accounting treatment even if the response form is not appropriately consistent with the appeal.

Challenge and matching gifts. Two of the relational giving patterns often used by charities are "challenge gifts" and "matching gifts." These tools have the potential for great benefit, but also for great misunderstanding, both to charities and to donors. A common meaning of the two terms are:

- **Challenge gifts.** A challenge gift is a *noncontingent* gift (not dependent on the gifts of other donors) to a charity with an accompanying "challenge" for other donors also to support the same charity. This is biblically portrayed through the Macedonia Church, which urgently encouraged others to give (2 Corinthians 8:3-5)."

  The challenge incentive is often used in television and radio fund-raising campaigns. Here are some examples:

  Example 1: "Bill Brown just called in and pledged $1,000 for the Sharathon. Bill *challenges* his friends and other listeners to join him in supporting this radio ministry by calling in your pledge in the next hour.

  Example 2: "A listener has committed a 'Dollar a Day' gift. It's an example that many can follow. We are *challenging* 30 other people to join him (or her) in the next hour. When you do, we'll have added more than $10,000 to our total."

  Example 3: "If you can give a gift of $500, now is a great time to call! A listener has committed a gift of $500 and we are *challenging* five other listeners to join him. We're looking for five people to give $500 in the next hour. We'll have added another $2,500 to the total if we accomplish this."

  The above examples do not use multiplier terminology; *e.g.*, "if you give $100, we will get $200." Instead, the examples use terminology making it clear the initial donor has committed to a noncontingency gift and if other donors pledge or give, the overall total is simply larger. Though it seems to be a technicality, it is fundamentally different from matching gifts in the fund-raising message.

- **Matching gifts.** A matching gift from a donor to a charity represents a gift that is *conditional or contingent* (dependent on the gifts of other donors) either in part or in whole (certain grants from one organization to another may be termed "matching" grants even though the grant is not contingent on gifts being raised. The grantor's requirements may be satisfied if the grant recipient's existing resources are identified and used as matching funds—see Examples 2 and 3 on pages 35-36.):

  ✓ gifts raised for one or more specific projects (restricted giving) or for unrestricted purposes, and/or

  ✓ gifts raised during a specific period of time.

  When a donor has made a matching gift commitment (one contingent on results), it should be based on a written statement or verbal dialogue concerning the terms of the matching gift.

  Example 1: "I have in my hand a matching-gift commitment for up to $3,000 from one of our listeners. It is not in our Sharathon total yet. This listener wants her *matching* gift to encourage others to join her in support of this station. For the next 30 minutes, she will *match* dollar for dollar up to her $3,000 offer. If you give in the next 30 minutes, your gift will effectively be doubled."

  Example 2: "Our ministry has a matching gift pledge from one of our loyal donors, who has committed to match gifts received by December 31 up to $50,000 for the building fund. This is a wonderful opportunity for you to double your gift to our ministry. Please send your check today with the enclosed response form."

Here are some of the integrity checkpoints for matching gifts:

✓ **The "at risk" element.** The fundamental basis of a matching gift from a donor to a charity is the *conditional* generosity of the matching-gift donor. If the matching gift is not at risk—the charity has already met the terms of the matching gift with internal funds or through some other means—there is no basis for a matching-gift communication with other donors.

Example 1: The donor writes a check to a charity for $50,000 and says: "If you can raise any matching gifts in relation to my gift, fine, but the $50,000 is yours." While this gift could be used as a challenge gift, it is not a matching gift. The $50,000 is not at risk and no matching-gift solicitation in connection with this gift is appropriate.

Example 2: A charity could use $250,000 of its unrestricted net assets to meet the matching requirements of a $250,000 government grant rather than soliciting the funds from its donors. The charity has sufficient resources to accommodate the match, satisfies the grant requirements, and receives the funds. If the charity sends a solicitation letter in reference to the matching gifts, the solicitation should clearly communicate that the terms of the matching gift have already been met, *i.e.*, the charity has already received all that it is eligible to receive from the matching-gift donor. The charity could ask for gifts to replace the unrestricted funds that were used to match the government grant making clear there is no multiplier impact because of a response to the general donor solicitation.

Example 3: A charity could use $250,000 of its unrestricted net assets to meet the matching requirements of a $250,000 government grant rather than soliciting the funds from its donors. Although the charity has sufficient assets to satisfy the requirements of the matching grant, the charity decides to raise gifts. The solicitation should clearly communicate that the charity could have used existing resources to satisfy the grant requirements, but the charity elected to raise gifts to qualify for the matching grant and, therefore, conserve existing resources. The solicitation letter should not use multiplier terminology (*e.g.,* "Your $100 gift will be matched dollar-for-dollar by the grant") because the charity could have satisfied the match using existing resources.

✓ **When the terms of a matching gift are not satisfied.** For the sake of integrity, funds from the initial matching-gift donor should not be accepted if the terms of the matching gift are not met. Example: A donor offers to give up to $100,000 for a certain project if the charity raises $100,000 within 90 days. The charity raises $90,000. The donor should only match $90,000 since these were the terms of the matching gift. If the donor wishes to make a later gift unrelated to the matching gift, it would be acceptable.

✓ **Tracking and remitting matching gifts.** Matching gifts require careful tracking in the donor management and accounting records. The terms of the matching-gift agreement with the initial donor should be precisely followed.

Often, matching-gift donors do not provide their gift to the charity until the charity has documented the total of the funds given in response to the matching gift. A detailed listing of gifts by donor should not be provided to the matching donor (this is private information) of the funds given related to the matching-gift appeal. In other instances, a matching-gift donor may provide a gift to the charity before funds have been raised. In these situations, the initial matching gift should be recorded as a liability until, or if, the funds are matched. Then a charitable gift receipt should be provided for the appropriate amount, *e.g.,* the total amount of the initial match should be receipted if the matching funds are fully raised, or the net amount of the initial matching gift if the matching funds are *not* fully raised and a partial refund is made to the donor.

✓ **When to receipt a matching gift.** If the matching gift is received by the charity before raising the additional funds, the donor's charitable receipt should be delayed until the charity fulfills the conditions of the gift.[13]

The proper handling of endowment gifts. An endowment fund may be established when a restricted gift is permanently set aside by a charity to fulfill a designated purpose. While the principal of the gift must generally be retained in the endowment fund and invested, the income from the principal is usually available for program purposes.

A donor may make an endowment gift to a charity by imposing certain restrictions on the gift. Or, an endowment fund may be established by action of the board of directors and donors may be asked to contribute to the fund. Many charities include an endowment component in fund-raising campaigns.

There may also be "term endowments" that are not permanently restricted but restricted for a specified period of time. At the end of the time period, the principal is then released for unrestricted or purpose restricted use as set forth in the agreement.

All charities should set aside cash operating reserves to protect against unexpected financial downturns. However, operating reserves are very different from endowments. An endowment should generally be invested for the long term compared to shorter-term investments for operating reserves. The Uniform Prudent Management of Institutional Funds Act (UPMIFA) applies to endowment funds but not to operating reserves (see pages 116-17). Endowments establish permanence for a charity.

An endowment fund is typically not a separate legal entity. It is simply a component of the charity, best evidenced by a board resolution. Its tax-exempt status is that of the charity itself. If a separate entity is established for the endowment, an independent tax-exemption determination will usually need to be obtained.

An endowment fund can be supportive of the entire range of programs of a charity or supportive of just one aspect of the organization. A charity can have multiple endowment funds.

It seems so simple to establish an endowment fund or accept an endowment gift, but this apparent simplicity belies many complex issues. Much of the confusion relates to terminology. The word endowment is often used too loosely and that may create problems. Plus, the qualifying terms that are used with the word endowment—pure, true, term, permanent and quasi—add to the complexity.

- **Types of endowments.** An endowment fund of cash, securities, or other assets provides income for the maintenance of a nonprofit organization. This implies the principal of the fund is segregated from other types of gifts to ensure the identity and integrity of the funds. Endowment requirements may not be met without distinct attention to the investment and spending of the endowment. This is generally demonstrated by establishing and following a separate investment use policy.

  It is possible for the assets of an endowment fund to be permanently restricted, temporarily restricted, or unrestricted in an accounting sense:

  ✓ **Permanently restricted.** Endowment funds may be established by donor-restricted gifts and bequests to provide a permanent (also referred to as pure or true) endowment, which provides a permanent source of income. Donor restrictions on such endowments are often respected in the law. Charity boards generally may not change the donor restrictions unless expressly granted such discretion in writing by the donor.

  The portion of a permanent endowment that must be maintained permanently—not used up, expended, or otherwise exhausted, is classified as *permanently-restricted net assets.*

  ✓ **Temporarily restricted.** An example of a temporarily restricted endowment fund is a term endowment, established to provide income for a specified period. For example, a donor might restrict the principal of the gift for ten years or until a certain event has occurred. Then, the donor might instruct that the principal may be reclassified as *unrestricted net assets.*

  ✓ **Unrestricted.** An organization's governing board may designate a portion of its unrestricted net assets as a board-designated endowment (sometimes referred to as funds functioning as endowment or quasi-endowment funds) to be invested to provide income for a long but unspecified period. A board-designated endowment, which results from an internal designation, is not donor-restricted and is classified as unrestricted net assets. Generally, the governing board has the right to decide at any time to expend the principal of such funds.

- **Determining donor intent.** Donor intent is often evidenced in one of the following ways:

  ✓ If a donor desires that the principal of a gift is to be maintained intact and in perpetuity, and only the income from the investment of the assets be expended, the donor may communicate these desires to the charity.

  ✓ The fund-raising communication between the charity and donor is often indicative of the nature of the gift. For example, if the charity establishes an endowment fund and a donor makes a gift in response to promotional material about the fund, a permanently restricted gift has been made.

- **Board authority over endowments.** The charity's board has authority in the following areas:

  ✓ To establish endowment policies that do not violate federal, state or local laws.

  ✓ Generally has the power to place unrestricted donations in an board designated (unrestricted) account.

  ✓ May have the power to allocate a portion of a temporarily or permanently restricted gift (representing allocable planned giving costs) for unrestricted purposes (including a board designated endowment fund).

  ✓ Generally has the power to direct the income from endowments (see next item).

- **Income from endowments.** Generally the earnings on an endowment fund itself are not restricted and can be used to carry out the charity's ongoing activities. However, some endowment gifts stipulate the uses to be made of the income—for example, for restricted purposes or programs.

Are endowment fund interest and dividends expendable? How about gains and losses? This depends on relevant law. It is often best for the gift agreement or solicitation to define what components of investment income are expendable for what purposes.

Since the principal may not be invaded unless the agreement provides for it, some nonprofits use a defined spending rate. If all gains, losses and income are expendable, they only spend, say, five percent of the endowment principal. This means that the unspent earnings are held as temporarily restricted. However, in a down market, it may be necessary for the organization to reduce the spending rate or subsidize from unrestricted funds since they cannot invade the principal.

- **Establishing endowment policies.** Before accepting endowment gifts, a charity's board should:

  ✓ Define the specific objectives the endowment fund must achieve for the charity.

  ✓ Decide whether or not to use a professional investment manager to mange the endowment fund

  ✓ Adopt a policy regarding the use of the endowment principal.

  ✓ Have its endowment policy and related forms prepared, or at least reviewed, by an attorney in the charity's state.

A charity's "endowment" policy should distinguish between quasi-endowment and endowment types of gifts. This clarification is very important for proper donor communications and to insure that the proper accounting treatment is followed for these gifts.

Does the charity's endowment policy have precedence over how donors understand the making of an endowment gift? For example, a charity's policy states: "Donations to the endowment fund shall be considered unrestricted, unless given for a specific purpose or for a specific term by the donor, which restrictions shall be set forth in a donor agreement between the donor and the charity." If this policy is communicated to donors, the policy will generally have precedence. But if the policy is not communicated, the donations to the endowment are restricted, which is consistent with the generally accepted meaning of the term "endowment."

- **Communicating with the donor.** Communications to donors should be consistent with the charity's policies. If funds are solicited for an endowment, the solicitation should clearly communicate if the gift principal will be invested with earnings used for operations or if the gifts will be used in some other way.

  What if fund-raising promotional materials state that, of the $25 million goal, $5 million will be used for endowment? However, the intent of the charity is to place the endowment gifts with their unrestricted net assets. Since the literature does not use unrestricted fund language, many donors would believe they are making permanently restricted gifts (based on the common definition of the word "endowment") of which only the earnings may be used for operations.

  If a charity promotes a gift-giving opportunity as one that "endows" a specific project or program and the charity plans to expend the gifts as they are received, it has misused the term "endowment." It is possible that donors could compel the charity to hold the funds as true or pure endowment. A contract or understanding and reliance by the donor may have inadvertently been created.

Chapter Review 3

1. Must a donor intend to benefit the charity for a gift to qualify as a charitable deduction? Yes. The donor's intent must be to benefit the charity and not an individual.

2. How does a donor explicitly restrict a gift? An explicit restriction occurs when the donor expresses gift restrictions in a direct and forthright manner. While an explicit restriction could be communicated verbally, restrictions are usually communicated in writing.

3. How does a donor implicitly restrict a gift? A restriction is implied if the circumstances surrounding the contribution make clear the donor's intended restriction on the use of the assets.

4. Is it possible for a donor to restrict a gift simply by placing a gift in the envelope that accompanies a particular appeal, even though no restriction was reflected on the check or on a response form? Yes. Placing a gift in an envelope that is identifiable with a certain appeal is an implicit gift restriction.

5. When is it appropriate to use the phrase "challenge gift?" When a gift is noncontingent—not dependent on the gifts of other donors.

6. When is it appropriate to use the phrase "matching gift?" When a gift is contingent—dependent on the gifts of other donors.

7. Should an organization that is considering establishing an endowment consult with an attorney in its state regarding policies and donation agreement forms? Yes.

Chapter 4

Restricted Funds that Cannot Be Used for the Intended Purpose

Executive Summary

- Under- or over-funding of projects or campaigns may leave a charity with funds which cannot be used for the purpose intended by the donor. These situations often require communication with the donors.
- Direct contact with donors is generally appropriate to discuss the possible redirection of significant restricted gifts. For gifts of more modest amounts, it may be appropriate to simply notify donors through a newsletter or email.
- For project or campaign balances of modest amounts, it may be appropriate to redirect the funds to a project with a similar purpose without communication with the donors.
- If a charity cannot fulfill a gift restriction and the restriction is not released or redirected, it may be appropriate to refund a gift to the donor.
- A disclaimer (explanation of how gifts will be used if a project or campaign is under- or over-funded) is often an appropriate communication to prospective donors.
- A disclaimer used in similar situations that is only communicated after a gift is given is generally not an effective notice to donors.
- A statement that the charity will exercise discretion and control with respect to a gift, although it may be an appropriate statement, does not release a charity from its responsibility to honor a donor's gift restriction.

Sometimes a charity holds temporarily- or permanently-restricted resources for which it has no use in the foreseeable future. This can occur either because the charity has accomplished the purpose for which the gifts were solicited and some amounts remained unspent, or there was an inability to proceed with a project for some reason (*e.g.,* the need no longer existed, there were political problems in the target country, the charity was unable to attract other needed resources, etc.). In this situation, the charity must decide what to do with the amount that cannot be used in the near future. (This discussion does not relate to refunds issued before the receipt is issued, *e.g.,* a credit card processing error.)

Options for the charity and the donor. These include the following.

- **Seek donor permission to redirect** the amounts to other projects or notify donors of the charity's intent to redirect gifts. Direct contact with donors is generally appropriate to discuss the redirection of significant restricted gifts. For gifts of more modest amounts, it may be appropriate to notify the donors through a letter, newsletter or email.

  Example 1: A charity raises gifts for a specific purpose. Hundreds of gifts of less than $100 each are received and one gift of $20,000 is received. The goal for the project was $50,000 and $65,000 was raised. Whether or not a disclaimer was communicated regarding the use of any contributions over the goal, at a minimum, the charity should contact the one major donor and seek permission to redirect the gift.

  Example 2: A charity raises gifts for a specific purpose. In the gift solicitation, the charity includes a disclaimer: "Gifts that exceed the amount needed for this project will be used for a similar project." The goal for the project was $25,000 and $26,000 was raised. The disclaimer statement generally gives the charity a right to redirect the $1,000 to a similar project without seeking donor permission.

  Example 3: A charity raises gifts for a specific purpose. In the gift solicitation, the charity *does not* include a disclaimer concerning any gifts that might be raised in excess of the goal for the project. The goal for the project was $25,000 and $30,000 was raised. Since the amount raised only exceeds the goal by $5,000, it may be appropriate to communicate the redirection of the excess gifts to project donors. If a donor contacts the charity and asks for a refund because the goal was exceeded, the charity should refund the portion of the gift represented by the excess amount raised ($5,000/$30,000 or 16.67%, in this example).

Example 4: A charity raises gifts for a specific purpose. In the gift solicitation, the charity includes a disclaimer: "Gifts that exceed the amount needed for this project will be used for a similar project." The goal for the project was $25,000 and $50,000 was raised. Since the amount raised exceeds the goal by a significant amount, the disclaimer is generally not effective to redirect the excess gifts. It is best to inform the donors of the amount received and communicate the planned use of the funds. If a donor contacts the charity and asks for a refund because the goal was exceeded, the charity should refund the portion of the gift represented by the excess amount raised ($25,000/$50,000 or 50%, in this example).

- **Seek a court order to redirect** the amounts without donor permission. This may be required for significant amounts only if the donor cannot be contacted.

Example: A donor makes a gift of $1 million dollars designated for a specified building project. The donor passes away without any heirs. The charity is unable to raise sufficient funds to construct the building. The charity seeks a court order to use the funds for other purposes.

The legal doctrines of *cy pres* and equitable deviation[14] have evolved to address situations when changed circumstances make it impossible for a charity to comply with gift restrictions:

- ✓ Courts (or state attorneys general) apply *cy pres* to restricted gifts when the designated charitable purpose becomes unlawful, impractical, or impossible to carry out, or it becomes wasteful to continue to apply the property to the designated charitable purpose. The doctrine permits the courts to alter the charitable purpose if the donor's original ones are no longer possible to achieve.[15]
- ✓ The equitable deviation doctrine addresses what happens when the means for carrying out a gift's purposes becomes impossible, impractical, illegal, obsolete, or ineffective.[16] This doctrine focuses on the restricted gift's administrative provisions rather than its purposes.

The court-administered *cy pres* and equitable deviation doctrines are often expensive to invoke because of legal fees and related costs and therefore generally only used for very large gifts. Applying for the *cy pres* doctrine is not a unilateral power of an organization's board. For example, an organization's board does not have the power to alter the charitable purpose if it is not possible to achieve the donor's original purpose—this power is reserved for courts or state attorneys general.

- **Redirect the amounts to a project with a similar purpose** if the amount involved is insignificant.

Example 1: A charity receives gifts for a specific purpose. Many years pass. The project is not completed and it is now impractical to complete it. The identity of the specific donors was not retained. It may be appropriate for the charity's board to redirect the funds for a similar purpose. If the amount of the gifts for this specific project are significant, it may be appropriate to include information about the planned redirection of the gifts in the charity's newsletter or other publication so that a donor to the project could express a desire about the use of his or her gift.

The above notice may have benefit in documenting that the statute of limitations is running. This would be particularly important if there were substantial gifts, and the charity has limited ability to determine who gave them. Aside from the legal benefit where there are delays in claiming the refund, some would recognize the moral argument that the organization has been transparent, and the donor has failed to pursue the issue in a timely manner.

Example 2: A charity receives many gifts for a specific purpose. The charity uses the funds for the specific purpose and there is an insignificant balance remaining in the specific purpose account. It may be appropriate for the charity's board or staff to redirect the funds for a similar purpose without contacting or notifying the donors as a matter of administrative discretion and practicality.

- **Refund unspent amounts to donors.** If a charity cannot fulfill a gift restriction and the restriction is not released or redirected, it may be appropriate to refund a gift to the donor.

Example 1: Five donors gave $1,000 each for a specific project that the charity does not complete. If the donors are unwilling to allow the redirection of their gifts for other purposes, the charity should refund the gifts to each of the donors.

Example 2: A charity announces a capital campaign to raise $25 million for a building and other purposes. Commitments are only received for $10 million resulting in significant changes to the building design and capacity. The charity fully informs donors of these campaign changes. Several donors want a refund of the gifts they have made and want their pledges cancelled because the campaign changes are so significant. The charity should refund the gifts to these individuals and cancel their pledges.

Refunding gifts to donors has implications for the charity's donor accounting records and the gift receipts. While a charity does not have any IRS filing requirement with respect to a gift refund, the refund of a donation may be taxable for a contribution that is refunded in a subsequent year[17] (see page 156). For a refund made in the same year in which it gift is received, a charity should notify the donor that a receipt issued for the gift is invalid and the charity should exclude the refunded gift from a year-end gift summary provided to the donor. A charity should communicate to the donor the potential tax implications of a refunded gift and encourage consultation with a tax professional.

Some charities include provisions in their governing documents or board resolutions indicating the organization retains the right to modify conditions on the use of assets (sometimes called "variance powers"). Such powers should be clearly communicated in writing to donors.[18]

It is common for boards of national charities with regional, state, or local subsidiary units to adopt variance powers with respect to estate gifts made to subsidiary units. For example, the national board may adopt variance power whereby a certain percentage of estate gifts made to subsidiary units may be used by the national organization or other subsidiaries on the premise that the credibility of the national organization has significant impact on a subsidiary being named as an estate beneficiary. The national and subsidiary organizations should make a reasonable effort to communicate such variance powers to potential donors.

The impact of disclaimers. It is often wise to include disclaimers (sometimes called "caveat" statements) with fund-raising appeals that will produce donor-restricted gifts. Unless disclaimers are used with appeals, a charity must consider limited options for handling excess project funding.

The following is a sample disclaimer that might accompany a restricted giving appeal: "All gifts are used as designated. However, in the unlikely event that a project becomes overfunded, your gift will be applied to a similar project." Or, the disclaimer might say "... your gift will be applied where needed most."

In the "applied to a similar project" example above, the overfunding of the first project would result in the funds remaining in the temporarily-restricted net assets class and used for a second project. However, in the "applied where needed most example," the donor restrictions would be released with respect to the overfunded amounts and the funds could be used for unrestricted purposes or left in the temporarily-restricted net asset class to fund another project.

For consistency with ECFA's Standards 7.1 Truthfulness in Communication, 7.2 Communication and Donor Expectations and 7.3 Communication and Donor Intent, disclaimer statements:

- should be communicated to donors in a manner that will be clearly understood (in other words, not printed in three-point font in a location only remotely related to the appeal) and
- are ineffective when it is expected that the appeal will raise significantly more than the amount needed for the particular project; *i.e.,* using an appeal expected to result in a significant overfunding to provide funds for less popular needs such as overhead expenses.

Disclaimer Example #1	
Appeal	Scholarship funds for summer youth camp
Disclaimer	Overfunding will be used where needed most
Financial Need	$50,000
Results of the fund-raising appeal	Raised $52,000 (about $50,000 is raised each year using a similar appeal)
Accounting Treatment	$50,000 for scholarships is recorded as temporarily-restricted revenue and $2,000 is recorded as unrestricted support
Comments on Example #1	The appeal and accounting treatment are appropriate in this example. The amount raised in excess of the need is immaterial.

Disclaimer Example #2	
Appeal	Scholarship funds for summer youth camp
Disclaimer	Overfunding will be used for books for camp library
Financial Need	$50,000
Results of the fund-raising appeal	Raised $60,000
Accounting Treatment	$50,000 for scholarships and $10,000 for camp library books is recorded as temporarily-restricted support
Comments on Example #2	The appeal and accounting treatment are appropriate in this example. The amount raised in excess of the need is material but the charity anticipated the overfunding and appropriately provided for it with the disclaimer.

<table>
<tr><th colspan="3">Disclaimer Example #3</th></tr>
<tr><td>Appeal</td><td colspan="2">Feed the homeless on Thanksgiving</td></tr>
<tr><td>Disclaimer</td><td colspan="2">Overfunding may be used where needed most</td></tr>
<tr><td>Financial Need</td><td colspan="2">$100,000 (based on the cost of food, food preparation, and applicable overhead)</td></tr>
<tr><td>Results of the fund-raising appeal</td><td colspan="2">Raised $250,000 (about $250,000 is raised each year using a similar appeal)</td></tr>
<tr><td>Accounting Treatment</td><td>How the charity recorded the gifts
• $100,000 was recorded as temporarily restricted for meals to be served on Thanksgiving
• $150,000 was recorded as unrestricted, based on the disclaimer</td><td>How the charity should have recorded the gifts
• $250,000 as temporarily restricted. The disclaimer was not effective in changing the nature of the temporarily-restricted gifts because:
1. The amount raised significantly exceeded need, and
2. The overfunding of the need should have been anticipated based on similar previous appeals.</td></tr>
<tr><td>Comments on Example #3</td><td colspan="2">This is an example of inappropriate use of a disclaimer in the fund-raising appeal. The amount raised in excess of the need is material and the charity should have anticipated the overfunding.</td></tr>
</table>

Chapter Review 4

1. Is it ever appropriate for a donor to unrestrict a previously restricted gift or to change a restriction after a gift is made? Generally, the only time this is appropriate is when a charity asks a donor to unrestrict a previously restricted gift or to change a restriction to allow use of the funds by the charity for another restricted purpose.

   A donor's unilateral request to change a restriction on a previously restricted gift is generally inappropriate. It would, in essence, change the "contract" for the use of the money. Additionally, it would perhaps give the donor the right to request a refund (if the charity can't or doesn't want to recognize the new restriction).

2. When is it appropriate for a charity to ask a donor to permit the redirection of a gift previously restricted by the donor? If a charity holds temporarily- or permanently-restricted resources for which it has no use in the foreseeable future, it is appropriate to seek donor permission to redirect the amounts to another project.

3. Is it ever appropriate for a charity to refund a gift to a donor? Yes. If a charity holds temporarily- or permanently-restricted resources for which it has no use in the foreseeable future and the charity has not obtained a release of the restriction or the right to redirect the funds for another use, it may be appropriate to refund a gift to the donor.

4. Is it appropriate to redirect gifts to another purpose when the gifts received exceed the project need and a disclaimer statement was made with the appeal? The disclaimer must be communicated to donors in a manner that will be clearly understood.

5. Are disclaimer statements always an effective way to give a charity the flexibility to use gifts for unrestricted purposes when the solicitation is for a project? No. Disclaimers are ineffective when an appeal is expected to result in a significant overfunding. For example, a charity has an annual appeal for the same project with a financial need for of $100,000. The prior year results of the appeal reflect gifts of $200,000 each year. A disclaimer stating that gifts received in excess of the amount needed for the project will be used for unrestricted purposes is an inappropriate use of a disclaimer. Diverting significant amounts of donor-restricted gifts through a simple disclaimer does not equate to proper and truthful communication to donors.

Chapter 5

Earmarked Gifts

Executive Summary

- When an amount is transferred to a charity with an accompanying obligation to benefit a particular individual, the charity may be assuming the role of an agent, with the amount transferred not qualifying for a charitable deduction.
- To be deductible, the charity must have discretion and control over a contribution without any obligation to benefit a designated individual.
- Gifts restricted for benevolence, scholarships and child adoption require special care to determine if the donor intends to benefit the charity or a particular individual and if the charity performs adequate discretion and control over the gifts.
- A special category of earmarked gifts occurs when a gift is passed through the charity for the donor's personal benefit. This could occur when a donor makes a gift to a charity restricted for the donor's (or donor's family) scholarship or child adoption. There is no charitable deduction for these gifts and should be rejected by charities.
- Since gifts by U.S. taxpayers to a foreign entity generally do not produce a charitable deduction, donors may earmark a gift for a foreign entity and try to convince a U.S. charity to pass it through to the foreign entity. This is generally inappropriate.
- Charities should generally turn down earmarked gifts since they are not in harmony with an organization's tax-exempt purpose. If accepted, no gift receipt should be provided.
- Gifts to a charity for the support of missionaries or other workers are generally not characterized as earmarked gifts, but tax-deductible contributions (see Chapters 7 and 8).

When preparing one's tax return, most taxpayers know that they cannot count tuition payments as a charitable deduction, even though the check is made out to a 501(c)(3) educational institution. In addition, most taxpayers know that their tuition payments are still not deductible if they are paid to a charity with instructions to forward the funds to the appropriate college or university.

Unfortunately, far too few donors and charities apply the same logic to other similar circumstances. In too many situations, it is generally accepted that when grants or gifts cannot be made directly, all one must do is 'launder' the money through a convenient 'fiscal agent,' which is frequently the local church or other charity."[19]

An earmarked gift is a transfer that has *not* been made to a charity in a deductible form because the recipient charity's function is as an agent for a particular noncharitable recipient.[20] The noncharitable recipient or beneficiary is often an individual, *e.g.*, a charity's worker (employee or independent contractor) or a benevolent recipient.

Sometimes providing financial assistance apart from a charity is desirable.

> ***Example:*** Jim, a college student and a counselor at a summer camp operated by a charity, accidentally rolls his old truck into a lake. The other counselors collect several hundred dollars and give the monies directly to Jim to help with the down payment for another truck. Since the counselors are making gifts to a particular individual, the use of the charity that operates the camp to receive gifts for Jim would not be appropriate. The counselors cannot claim tax deductions for their gifts to Jim. However, Jim is not subject to federal income tax on the gift amount. The other counselors would not be subject to federal gift tax if the total gifts made by each counselor to Jim during the year did not exceed the annual exclusion amount.

Here are a few examples of the improper attempts to use a charity as a *fiscal agent* in an effort to obtain a charitable deduction:

> "I want to help my friends, Fred and Mary, who are going through a tough financial time because of a recent hurricane.

> I realize they have no connection with your organization but if I give the charity $500, will you pass it through to them and give me a charitable receipt?"
>
> "I want to give $10,000 to the church so the funds can be passed on to a college to cover the tuition for the pastor's daughter. Will the church process this gift and give me a receipt?"
>
> "I want to give $5,000 to your charity for the equal distribution to five specific office staff whom I will identify."
>
> "I want to give $1,000 to the church for benevolence with the understanding that $500 will be given to the Brown family, who have a significant financial need."

Examples like these are donations "earmarked" for individuals. They are also called "conduit" or "pass-through" transactions. These connotations are negative references when used by the Internal Revenue Service (IRS) and generally denote amounts that do not qualify for a charitable deduction.[21] To be deductible, the charity must have discretion and control over a contribution without any obligation to benefit a designated individual.[22] The donor's motivation may be loving and charitable in a broad sense; the donor wants to help, and the only problem is the donor's desire for control.

Identifying an earmarked gift. A tell-tale sign of an earmarked (or conduit or pass-through) gift is when someone says they want to "run a gift through the charity," "pass a gift through the charity," or "process a gift through the charity." Of course, it is possible the donor will not so clearly signal an earmarked gift and use more general terminology. This is why charities should have a good understanding on the concept of earmarked gifts in addition to an awareness of tell-tale terminology.[23]

Though the concept in tax law is well-established, it can be hard to apply to specific situations. Savvy charity leaders will establish and follow clear policies to prohibit donors from passing money through the ministry simply to gain a tax benefit. The following examples illustrate the difference between a deductible restricted gift and a nondeductible earmarked gift:

Example 1: A potential donor says, "If your charity won't process this gift restricted for Nancy Smith, I know of another charity that will handle it," thus implying they will look for another charity with less stringent gift policies. This type of communication demonstrates the donor's desire to benefit a designated individual and not to benefit a charity. This potential transfer of funds to a charity should not be accepted.

Example 2: Sometimes the difference between a non-deductible conduit gift and a deductible restricted gift is not who benefits but only who determines the beneficiary. For example, Mary Smith gave a $500 gift to a church benevolence fund indicating a preference that the benevolent recipient be Ruth Phillips. Clarice Jones gave $500 to the same church with a restriction that the money go to Ruth Phillips. In the first example, after proper consideration, the church benevolence committee designated Ruth Phillips as the beneficiary of $500. This fact pattern is generally consistent with a deductible gift. The second example is a nondeductible conduit gift that generally should not be accepted by the church. The potential beneficiary was the same in both examples, demonstrating the principle that it is not who benefits but who determines the beneficiary that may determine the propriety for such a transaction.

Though many charitable donations are based on a sense of charity, selflessness, and even love, the IRS believes that people may also have other motivations. The law prevents donors from having undue influence over charities and restricts donors from manipulating a charity into serving noncharitable interests and receiving a deduction for it at the same time.

A special category of earmarked gifts occurs when a a gift is passed through the charity for the donor's personal benefit (also called "roundtripping"). Scholarship gifts passed through a charity for the donor's children (instead of paying tuition) fall into this category of gifts for a donor's personal benefit and may raise allegations of tax fraud. Gifts by a donor to purchase life insurance on the donor benefiting the donor's family resulted in a law which can cause substantial penalties for both the donor and organization.[24] Contributions to a qualified charity earmarked for an unqualified donee may raise a question as to qualifying for a charitable deduction.[25]

Gifts to a charity for the support of missionaries or other workers (often called "deputized fund-raising") are subject to a different set of guidelines (see Chapter 7) than those generally associated with earmarked gifts. Gifts made under a properly structured deputized fund-raising program are generally tax deductible to the donor.

What tests can a charity use to determine whether it should consider accepting a gift that may be an earmarked gift? Here are three questions the charity may ask:

1. **What are the donor's intentions?** The donor's intent in making the payment must be to benefit the charity and not the individual recipient.

2. **Does the gift benefit an indefinite group?** Indefiniteness is often an essential element of a charitable gift.[26] Earmarking or designating individual donees lacks the element of indefiniteness. The indefiniteness standard is satisfied if the charity retains control of the funds. A pool of potential beneficiaries must be sufficiently large or indefinite that it constitutes a charitable class. Even when contributions are restricted by the donor to a class of beneficiaries, the class of potential beneficiaries may still be too narrow to qualify as a deductible charitable contribution.[27]

   One court observed: "Charity begins where certainty in beneficiaries ends, for it is in the uncertainty of the objects and not in the mode of relieving them which forms the essential element of charity."[28] When a beneficiary is designated by name, the gift is private, not public, and does not have the characteristics of a charitable gift.

3. **How much discretion and control does the charity have over the contribution?** This test focuses on the amount of discretion and control the charity has over the contribution:

- An important element for the donor of a charitable contribution is the donee's control over the donated funds. It must be shown that the charity retained control over the funds. To have control of donated funds is to have discretion over their use.

- In instances where a donor designates a gift to benefit a particular individual and the individual does benefit from the gift, the determination of whether the gift is deductible depends upon whether the charity has full control of the donated funds and discretion over their use.

- If contributions are earmarked by the donor for a particular individual and the charity exercises no control or discretion over their use, they are treated as gifts to the designated individual and are not deductible as charitable contributions.[29]

As with all charitable contributions, restricted gifts must be *for the use* of a charity.[30] One court concluded that "for the use of" means roughly the equivalent of "in trust for."[31]

With respect to all charitable gifts, a charity must have control over the funds and discretion over their use. It must determine whether the proposed use of the money furthers its own charitable purposes. The charity may actually use the funds in the exact way the donor intended, but because the charity exercises adequate due diligence over the gift and selects the ultimate recipient in a totally independent manner, the transaction may avoid the earmarked label.

Accepting and receipting earmarked gifts. In certain instances, charities accept gifts that are clearly earmarked, *i.e.,* the discretion and control factors are not present for a certain benevolent recipient. For example:

- A donor may desire to make an earmarked gift to assist a needy individual, but the donor wants to make an anonymous gift. The charity accepts the payment with the understanding that no charitable gift receipt will be issued. For accounting purposes, it is treated as an agency transaction, excluded from revenue and expense.

- Organizations conducting international operations sometimes accept funds that do not represent charitable contributions and transfer the funds to the charity's workers located in parts of the world where banking options are limited. These "personal" gifts are accepted because it may be difficult for friends and family to transfer funds to the worker without the assistance of the charity. For accounting purposes, these gifts are treated as an agency transaction, excluded from revenue and expense.

Charities should generally avoid accepting earmarked gifts and transferring them to a benevolent recipient or to the charity's worker outside the charity's compensation reporting system because of these potential issues:

- **For the charity.** It is difficult to justify accepting and disbursing earmarked gifts since, by their nature, they are not in harmony with an organization's tax-exempt purpose. Additionally, treating the disbursement of funds as earmarked gifts to workers and not including the amounts on the worker's Form W-2 or 1099-MISC could be considered private benefit or inurement.

  Most missionaries have U.S. bank accounts to which personal funds may be deposited. The missionaries can then draw on the funds through cash machines, deposits to international bank accounts, or using other banking techniques.

  The mere handling of earmarked gifts requires the use of certain tax-exempt resources for nontax-exempt purposes, adding to the reasons why earmarked gifts should generally not be accepted.

- **For the donor.** Earmarked gifts are generally not deductible as a charitable contribution. However, it would be possible for donors of single gifts for personal purposes of less than $250 to simply use their cancelled checks to substantiate an inappropriately claimed charitable deduction. Therefore, simply by depositing a personal gift, a charity may unwittingly assist a donor in claiming a charitable deduction to which he or she is not entitled. Thus, if an earmarked gift of less that $250 is handled by a charity, the charity should stamp "Not a Charitable Gift" across the face of the check so the cancelled check cannot be used to substantiate a charitable deduction.

Types of earmarked gifts. The following types of gifts are especially at risk of being classified as earmarked gifts unless they are properly handled:

- **Benevolence gifts.** Benevolence gifts are given to needy individuals or families. Benevolence gifts made directly by a donor to needy individuals are not deductible.[32] To qualify for a charitable deduction, contributions must be made to a qualified organization.

  It is generally preferable for a charity to make benevolence gifts from the charity's general fund or from a benevolence fund based on gifts restricted for the benevolence fund but not preferenced for a particular benevolent recipient. Gifts to benevolent recipients should follow policies established to determine worthy recipients of benevolence funds. These practices will form a sound basis for handling benevolence funds and help insure the deductibility of gifts given to a charity for benevolent purposes.

  Contributions to a benevolence fund may generally be claimed as charitable deductions. If a donor makes a suggestion about the beneficiary of a benevolent contribution, it may be deductible if the recipient organization exercises proper control over the benevolence fund. The suggestion must only be advisory in nature and the charity may accept or reject the gift.

  It is often helpful for charities to form a benevolence committee for the express purpose of determining the recipients of the benevolence funds and the amounts they should receive.

  Benevolence to "insiders" requires additional consideration. Insiders are individuals with a personal and private interest in the activities of the nonprofit. Insiders may include the top executives, senior pastor, members of the governing board, officers, the founder, substantial contributors, certain employees, and family members of these individuals. Private inurement occurs whenever assets of the organization are used to benefit of insiders rather than in the mission of the organization. Thus, benevolence money given to an insider may violate the private inurement requirement and trigger the intermediate sanction rules.[33]

  In general, all economic benefits provided to an employee are taxable compensation unless specifically excluded by statute.[34] However, the IRS may presume that payments made by a charity to its employees or their family members for disaster relief (also see pages 130-32) and emergency hardship are consistent with the charity's exempt purpose, and neither taxable compensation to the employee nor private inurement, if (1) the potential class of beneficiaries is large or indefinite, (2) the recipients are selected based on an objective determination of need, and (3) the selection is made using an independent selection committee.[35]

Benevolence payments to nonemployees are *not* reportable on Form 1099-MISC (or any other information form).[36] Benevolence payments to employees are generally reportable on Form W-2 unless three criteria stated in the previous paragraph are satisfied.

- **Scholarship gifts.** Charities can provide scholarships to further the educational endeavors of individuals. Donations to a scholarship fund that are not designated for a particular student or that benefits an "indefinite class" of beneficiaries generally qualify as charitable deductions. (There must be a sufficient number of potential beneficiaries to meet the indefinite class definition.)

  A charity should adopt appropriate guidelines to protect the contributor's tax deduction for gifts to a scholarship fund:

  ✓ The charity determines all scholarship recipients through the use of a scholarship committee.

  ✓ The charity has a well-published policy that it determines the recipients, according to its own policies, and it expressly rejects any effort to honor a donor's recommendations.

  ✓ Recipients of scholarships and the amount they are to receive are based on funds already received.

  ✓ The criteria for scholarship qualification are in writing.

  ✓ Scholarship policies contain the following statement: "Scholarships are awarded without regard to sex, race, nationality, or national origin."

When donors designate a gift to a private or church-affiliated school for a particular student, especially if the student is a family member, no charitable deduction is typically allowed because the gift is earmarked.[37] A charitable contribution is "a voluntary transfer of money or property that is made with no expectation of procuring a financial benefit commensurate with the amount of the transfer."[38] Therefore, payments made to a school are considered to be made in exchange for providing educational services to a named relative. Since the charity is obligated to provide the education to—or use the funds for a scholarship for—the named student, the donor received a benefit presumed to be equal to the amount contributed.

The IRS approved an exception to the nondeductible-tuition rule where contributions are designated for a specific program and selection of recipients is beyond the donor's control.[39]

Scholarships for dependents of employees represent taxable compensation to the employee unless they meet certain precise guidelines.[40] The requirements include:

1. The existence of the program must not be presented as a benefit of employment by the organization.
2. Selection of beneficiaries must be made by an independent committee.
3. Selection must be based solely upon substantial objective standards that are completely unrelated to the employment of the recipients or their parents and to the employer's line of business.
4. Generally, not more than 25% of eligible dependents may be recipients of scholarships.

- **Child adoption gifts.** It is not surprising that charities and donors often seek ways to provide financial support to couples involved in the adoption process. The cost to adopt a child often exceeds the financial resources of the adopting couple.

  While there are a few ways charities can legitimately assist adoptive parents, these options are very limited. A charity should carefully scrutinize any gifts that are designated for a particular adoptive family. The IRS may consider such gifts as conduit or pass-through transactions which do not qualify for a charitable receipt by a charity or a charitable deduction by a donor and could endanger the tax status of a charity.

The following are some considerations for providing support for adoptive parents:

- ✓ **Personal gifts to the adoptive parents.** An individual may make a personal gift to adoptive parents to assist with adoption expenses. Personal gifts are not deductible as charitable gifts and are not taxable to the adoptive parents.

- ✓ **Gifts for adoptive parents by a charity whose purpose and nature are not consistent with such gifts.** If gifts by a charity to adoptive families are not consistent with the broad limits imposed by the charity's purpose and nature, the gifts are generally not a proper use of tax-exempt funds.

- ✓ **Gifts for adoptive parents from the operating fund of a charity.** If adoption assistance is consistent with the charity's purpose and nature, a charity generally has a sound basis to provide assistance for adoptive parents from the charity's general funds (budgeted or unbudgeted); *e.g.,* the charity has available funds that were not designated by a donor for a particular adoptive family. Payments for adoptive families are often made on the basis of financial need and paid directly to the adoption agency to assure that the funds are properly used. These payments are tax-free to the adopted parents.[41]

- ✓ **Gifts to a charity's adoption fund not preferenced for a particular adoptive family and gifts for an adoptive family from the fund.** If adoption assistance is consistent with the charity's purpose and nature, a charity generally has a sound basis to establish a restricted fund (either temporarily restricted or permanently restricted) to accept gifts that are not designated by a donor for a particular adoptive family. Gifts to such a fund will generally qualify as charitable gifts. Payments for adoptive families are often made on the basis of financial need. Payments should typically be made directly to the adoption agency or reimbursed to the adoptive parents based on adequate documentation to assure that the funds are properly used.

- ✓ **Gifts to a charity preferenced for a particular adoptive family and gifts for the adoptive family from the fund.**

Providing Assistance to or for Adoptive Parents

Implications for ECFA Standards and Charitable Deduction Purposes

Type of Gift	Complies with ECFA Standards	Qualifies as a Charitable Deduction
Gift from a charity to/for an adoptive family based on need[(1) (2)] – not based on gifts designated by the donor(s), *e.g.*, from the charity's general fund	Yes	Yes
Gift from a charity to/for an adoptive family based on gifts restricted for the charity's adoption fund but not restricted or preferenced for a particular adoptive family.	Yes	Yes
Personal gifts from one individual to/for another individual to assist in an adoption.	Not Applicable	No
Gift from a charity to/for an adoptive family based on gifts preferenced for a particular adoptive family and the donor's intent is to benefit the adoptive family, not the charity.	No. Violates ECFA's Standard 7.8	No
Gift from a charity to/for an adoptive family based on gifts restricted for a particular adoptive family. *The charity is unable to provide adequate control and discretion over the payment because of the donor(s) restriction.*	No. Violates ECFA's Standard 7.8	No
Gift from a charity to/for an adoptive family based on gifts restricted for a particular adoptive family – the adoptive family and the donor are the same taxpayer.	No. Violates ECFA's Standard 7.8	Generally, no. May be tax fraud because of the circular nature of the transaction
Gift from a charity to/for an adoptive family based on gifts preferenced for a particular adoptive family. *The charity exercises adequate control and discretion over the gift.*	Based on facts and circumstances	Based on facts and circumstances

(1) As a best practice, the payments should either be made directly to the adoption agency or reimbursed to the adoptive parents based on adequate documentation to assure that the funds are properly used.

(2) Personal gifts from an individual to another individual may have estate tax implications if the gifts to an individual exceed the annual gift tax limitation.

Even if adoption assistance is consistent with the charity's governing documents, gifts that are preferenced by a donor for a particular adoptive family may raise conduit or pass-through transaction issues. To be deductible, the charity must generally have control and discretion over the contribution without any obligation to benefit a preferenced individual, obtain adequate information about the potential recipient of the funds (including financial resources), avoid refunding gifts to donors if a particular adoption is not completed, and avoid conflicts of interest between those approving and receiving a loan or a grant.[42] Before considering accepting gifts of this nature and making related gifts to adoptive parents, a charity should seek qualified legal counsel.

- **Foreign charity gifts.** Earmarked gifts are not limited to gifts earmarked for individuals; a gift may be earmarked for an organization. It may be inappropriate to accept gifts restricted for a foreign charity even if the charitable purposes of the foreign charity are consistent with the purposes of the U.S. charity.[43]

Example 1: An individual offers to make a $5,000 donation to a charity (Sri Lanka Relief Outreach) restricted for the relief and development purposes of a foreign charity. While the recipient charity provides funding for various foreign missionary endeavors, it has no connection with the Sri Lanka Relief Outreach and has no practical way, directly or indirectly, to provide due diligence in relation to a gift to this entity. Based on these facts, the gift has the characteristics of an earmarked gift. The funds should generally not be accepted by the charity.

Example 2: Same fact pattern as in Example 1, except the charity regularly sponsors short term mission trips to Sri Lanka and provides funds to the Sri Lanka Relief Outreach, based on the due diligence performed by the charity's staff and volunteers on mission trips with respect to this particular foreign entity. Based on these facts, the charity is generally in a sound position to make a gift of $5,000 to the

Sri Lanka-based charity as requested by the donor, avoiding the characteristics of earmarking.

Since gifts by U.S. taxpayers to a foreign entity do not produce a charitable deduction, unless permitted by a tax treaty,[44] donors may earmark a gift for a foreign entity and try to convince a U.S. charity to pass it through to the foreign entity. When a domestic charity is empowered in such a way that it is no more than an agent of or trustee for a particular foreign organization, has purposes so narrow that its funds can go only to a particular foreign organization; or solicits funds on behalf of a particular foreign organization, the deductibility of gifts may be questioned by the IRS.[45]

There are some acceptable situations where a U.S. charity may receive gifts for which a deduction is allowed with the money used abroad:

- ✓ The money may be used by the U.S. charity directly for projects that it selects to carry out its own exempt purposes. In this instance, the domestic organization would generally have operations in one or more foreign countries functioning directly under the U.S. entity. The responsibility of the donee organization ends when the purpose of the gift is fulfilled. A system of narrative and financial reports is necessary to document what was accomplished by the gift.

- ✓ It may create a subsidiary organization in a foreign country to facilitate its exempt operations there, with certain of its funds transmitted directly to the subsidiary. In this instance, the foreign organization is merely an administrative arm of the U.S. organization, with the U.S. organization considered the real recipient of the contributions. The responsibility of the U.S. organization ends when the purpose of the gift is fulfilled by the foreign subsidiary.

- ✓ It may make grants to charities in a foreign country in furtherance of its exempt purposes, following review and approval of the uses to which the funds are to be put. The responsibility of the U.S. organization ends when the purpose of the gift is fulfilled by the foreign organization. A narrative and financial report from the foreign organization will usually be necessary to document the fulfillment of the gift.

✓ It may transfer monies to another domestic entity with the second organization fulfilling the purpose of the gift. The responsibility of the first entity usually ends when the funds are transferred to the second organization.

The tax law is clear that money given to an intermediary charity but earmarked for an ultimate recipient is considered to have been given directly to the ultimate recipient. It is earmarked if there is an understanding, written or oral, whereby the donor binds the intermediary charity to transfer the funds to the ultimate recipient. The tax law does not allow donors to accomplish indirectly through a conduit (an intermediary charity) what the donor cannot accomplish directly.

Earmarked gifts and donor advised funds. Some donors to DAFs try to use another organization to earmark a gift. Use of an organization for an earmarked gift by a DAF is essentially a type of non-exempt activity and potentially even fraudulent. If it was illegal for the DAF to directly make the gift, then simply acting as a conduit intentionally hides an illegal act to avoid adverse tax consequences.

Subsequent to the passage of the Pension Protection Act of 2006:

- The donor to a DAF can no longer influence use of the funds for individuals either by direct payment or indirectly by passing it through a "helpful" church or other organization.
- The donor to a DAF continues to be able to influence use of the funds to an exempt purpose or project (such as evangelism, feeding the poor, or benevolence).
- A tax-exempt organization receiving funds from a DAF for a specified purpose, project, or general benevolence can, through the exercise of its control and discretion, use those funds to pay employees or other expenses, or make gifts or grants to accomplish the project or benevolence.

In some instances, modifying the earmarked element can make the transaction legitimate. Essentially, in all of the following examples, the organization asserts full control over the grant, making the grant effectively part of its exempt resources. Some examples are:

- Where previously the DAF directly supported a specific foreign worker, the DAF donor makes a grant to a U.S. tax exempt mission organization working in that part of the world, and only requests that it be used for evangelism in that country. Where the mission organization already works in the country, it may accept the gift with that restricted purpose.
- Where previously the donor to a DAF used the funds to provide meals directly to homeless people in the donor's home town, the DAF donor makes a gift to a local rescue mission, restricted to providing meals. Where the rescue mission already provides meals, it may accept the gift with that restricted purpose.
- Where a donor to a DAF previously gave money to help a specific unrelated, impoverished person to pay rent, the DAF donor could make a gift to a church which had an organized benevolence program. If the gift was irrevocable regardless of whether the recommended person was helped, the church may accept the gift restricted for its benevolence program.

In all of these examples, there can be no "side understandings." It does not matter whether the understanding is legally enforceable or not. The essence of a DAF is the donor's ability to make recommendations. It is essential that in all of these situations there be no expectation that the donor will have direction of the final use of the funds beyond the broad area designation or restriction for a specific exempt purpose or project.

In addition to the penalties associated with improper DAF distributions, organizations facilitating pass-through/conduit distributions from DAFs risk private inurement and private benefit violations. In essence, they are allowing a very valuable resource, their tax status, to be used for private benefit.

The following examples are not consistent with the necessary discretion and control over the gifts that must be demonstrated by the charity.

- Communications regarding missionary fund-raising may suggest that contributions are supporting the missionary as an individual.

- Organizational materials may emphasize the organizations faithfulness to follow donor's designations, without corresponding emphasis of the organizations' control to assure that funds are used for the organizations goals and purposes.
- Missionary newsletters may refer to donors as "supporting the missionary" rather than supporting the mission.

Since a DAF cannot make grants to a person, or even pay a person's expenses, if the sponsoring organization of a DAF believes the DAF is making grants to an individual (even if mistaken), it may stop them until the transaction is clarified.

Most organizations that raise support for worker ministries (deputized fund-raising), however, properly exercise supervision and control over all contributions raised by their workers. The contribution is not to the individual. The charity is not acting as a conduit or pass-through.

The key is providing proper communication. This should start with the review of organizational materials and worker communications. Targeted communication with the sponsoring organization of the DAF may be helpful. Perhaps a useful question would be, "Does your communication as a whole (including worker letters and reports) emphasize the organization's stewardship and control over funds raised by workers, or does it emphasize (perhaps by silence) the organization's passivity regarding these funds?"

In principle, if gifts to support the ministry of individual workers are fully under the control of the exempt organization and meet IRS guidelines, such gifts should be proper as long as the individual workers are not related to the donor. However, if gifts are in substance an earmarked transaction that benefits an individual without proper oversight and control by the recipient organization, the gift may not be deductible by the donor and may create problems for a DAF.[46]

Chapter Review 5

1. Why is it important to determine whether a particular gift is earmarked for a certain individual? Earmarked gifts generally should not be accepted by a charity (and, if accepted, not receipted as a charitable gift) because they do not represent resources that are consistent with a charity's tax-exempt status.

2. What incentive does a donor have to earmark a gift for a foreign charity? Gifts by U.S. taxpayers to a foreign charity do not produce a charitable deduction. However, a donor may claim an inappropriate charitable deduction based on convincing a U.S. charity to accept a gift earmarked for a foreign charity.

3. How may a charity identify an earmarked gift before receiving the funds? It is generally a matter of determining if the donor intends to benefit the charity (and an indefinite group of beneficiaries) or an individual, and how much control the donor desires over the gift.

4. How can gifts avoid the earmarked label? If a donor intends to benefit the charity, restricts the gift for an indefinite group of beneficiaries and the charity provides significant discretion and control over the gift, the transaction may avoid the earmarked label.

5. Should a charity accept an earmarked gift even if a gift receipt is not provided? Generally, no. It is difficult to justify accepting and disbursing earmarked gifts since earmarked gifts are not in harmony with an organization's tax-exempt purpose.

6. May a donor to a DAF influence use of the funds for individuals? No. This is not permitted, either by direct payment or indirectly by passing it through a "helpful" church or other organization.

Chapter 6

Overhead Assessed on Restricted Gifts

Executive Summary

- Overhead assessments may often be legitimately made to donor-restricted gifts to offset a charity's fund-raising and general and administrative expenses.
- A donor may stipulate that a gift may not be used for overhead costs. While the charity could reject the gift, if the gift is accepted, the charity must comply with the donor's conditions.
- Various methods are used by charities to determine overhead amounts charged to donor-restricted gifts. Whether an arbitrary rate is applied or the rate is based on cost analysis, overhead charges must never exceed actual overhead costs.
- The law generally does not require that a charity disclose the administrative costs charged to restricted donations. However, disclosure of an overhead assessment policy demonstrates a charity's transparency.
- When a donor-restricted gift is made to a charity, 100 percent of the gift should be recorded as restricted (either temporarily or permanently restricted) even when the charity applies an overhead assessment to the gift. To satisfy the donor's restriction, the overhead assessment should be reclassified from restricted to unrestricted.

Overhead assessments are often applied to restricted donations by a charity. Since there is generally a cost involved in soliciting donations, it's plausible to either charge a restricted project with fund-raising expenses or include a fund-raising expense component as part of an administrative fee. Likewise, it is often reasonable to allocate certain general and administrative costs to the projects and programs for which the funds are raised.

Donors generally understand that overhead is required to solicit gifts as well as to carry out the related program purpose funded by the gifts. However, there is probably less comprehension that overhead amounts are sometimes deducted from restricted gifts. It is important for a charity to appropriately determine donor expectations and donor intent for all restricted gifts, including the application of overhead assessments to these gifts, being mindful of ECFA's Standard 7.2 (communication and donor expectations) and 7.3 (communication and donor intent).

If a charity desires to utilize the overhead assessment concept, the proactive adoption of board or administrative polices to structure the arrangement is fundamental. It is also important to provide for proper accounting of assessments and periodically determine that the overhead rates do not exceed actual costs.

Overhead charges must never exceed actual overhead costs, whether an arbitrary rate is applied or if the rate is based on cost analysis. Applying this principle requires the determination of overhead costs (perhaps based on the most recent audited financial statement) before the overhead assessment fee is established. Overhead charges should generally be established based on actual experience instead of budgetary projections.

Limitations on the application of overhead assessments on restricted gifts. The following are the primary limitations on applying overhead assessments to restricted gifts:

- **State laws.** Certain state laws could apply in situations where a charity accepts a restricted gift and applies an overhead assessment that exceeds applicable costs, expending less than the appropriate amount for the donor-restricted purpose. ECFA's Standard 4 requires the use of resources in conformity with applicable laws.

- **Donor restrictions.** When a donor makes a gift to a charity, the gift may be conditional on no overhead assessment being applied to the gift. If a charity accepts a gift with such a condition, no overhead charge may be made against the gift to keep faith with the donor's restriction.

- **Statements by a charity.** At times, a charity states that no overhead assessments will be applied to gifts because overhead costs have been underwritten by a specific gift or gifts for that purpose. If such a statement is made, it is improper to apply an overhead assessment to restricted gifts.

Determining an appropriate rate for the overhead assessment. Determining whether to apply an overhead assessment on restricted gifts is a discretionary matter for a charity. Some charities elect not to apply an overhead assessment on restricted gifts. Other charities choose to apply an overhead assessment, or a partial assessment, to certain gifts. The level of the assessment applied may relate to the public perception of how certain gifts will be used (*e.g.*, in disaster-relief fund-raising, donors may believe that few, if any, overhead deductions will be made) or may relate to a variety of other factors. While there is no standard overhead assessment, rates in the 5-20 percent range are common. It is important for organizations to adopt clear and consistent overhead assessment practices that are reasonable.

There are some practices for determining what is charged to donor-restricted gifts:

- Only direct program or project costs

- Direct program costs plus fund-raising costs

- Direct program costs plus an administrative assessment

- Direct program costs plus fund-raising costs and an administrative assessment or an assessment that includes fund-raising costs

The following considerations may apply in determining the maximum administrative assessment:

1. **The fund-raising component.** Compare expenses allocated to fund-raising to total cash and noncash contributions to

determine the fund-raising component of the assessment. In theory, the fund-raising expenses allocable to raising each segment of restricted gifts, purpose-by-purpose, would represent the most accurate fund-raising assessment rate.

A more generalized approach compares fund-raising expenses to total expenses to determine the fund-raising rate of the assessment.

2. **The general and administrative component.** Ideally, the general and administrative expenses relating to carrying out a program funded by restricted gifts would compare to the applicable restricted gifts, perhaps even program-by-program. This level of sophisticated expense allocation is rarely possible.

   Often used is the more generalized approach of comparing total general and administrative expenses to total expenses to determine the general and administrative rate of assessment.

Communicating the overhead assessment to the donor. Disclosure to donors of administrative assessments charged to restricted donations is generally not required by law. Some ministries practice this disclosure while others do not. Disclosing an overhead assessment policy demonstrates maximum transparency. The overhead assessment policy could be disclosed in fund-raising solicitations or published in periodicals that describe donor-restricted giving possibilities: in newsletters, on websites, and/or in brochures that are sent to donors about the organization's policies and practices (a sample communication regarding an organization's overhead is on page 138).

If an overhead charge is assessed, the fund-raising solicitations and any other communications with donors should not leave the donor with the impression that no overhead charge will be made against the gift.

Accounting for overhead assessments. Charities should record 100 percent of a restricted gift in the applicable classification of restricted gift revenue (temporarily or permanently restricted) and then the overhead assessment is reclassified to unrestricted from the applicable restricted classification (either in concert with satisfying restrictions, or as the funds are raised without regard to whether the restrictions have yet been satisfied). This recording is done on the premise that the entire gift is initially restricted.

Recording the administrative assessment as unrestricted revenue in the accounting records when the gift is received on the premise that the administrative assessment portion of the gift is unrestricted is only appropriate when donors have expressly identified the administrative assessment as an unrestricted gift.

Disclosing administrative assessment charging policies in the notes to the financial statements is an excellent practice, including stating whether the overhead charges are reflected in unrestricted revenue or initially shown in restricted revenue and then reclassified.

Chapter Review 6

1. May charities apply an overhead assessment on restricted donations? Generally, yes, unless: the donor has expressly stated otherwise, the charity has committed not to apply an overhead assessment to the gift(s), or state law restricts the application of an overhead assessment.

2. What is the preferred method to establish an overhead assessment which will be applied to certain restricted donations? Overhead charges should generally be established based on actual experience, often based on the charity's most recent audited financial statement. If budgetary projections are used as a basis for overhead assessments, adjustments to the assessment rate should be subsequently made.

3. Should a charity communicate its overhead assessment practice to donors? Although this is generally not required, many charities proactively communicate overhead practices in an annual report or other periodic communication to donors.

4. When an overhead assessment is applied to restricted gifts, does this change the revenue classification of the initial gift? No. The entire restricted gift should be classified as temporarily or permanently restricted. Then, on the statement of activities, the overhead assessment is reclassified to unrestricted from the applicable restricted classification.

Chapter 7

Contributions to Support Missionaries and Other Workers

Executive Summary

- For a contribution to a charity for the support of a particular missionary or another specific worker to qualify for a charitable deduction, often called "deputized fund-raising," the gift must only be preferenced for the support of the individual, not restricted to benefit a certain individual.
- All funds raised by workers under the deputized fund-raising concept are solely to accomplish the charitable purposes of the charity. The workers are only representatives of the charity.
- The donor's intent must be to benefit the charity and not an individual. Communicating to a potential donor that the charity will have complete discretion and control over donor-preferenced gifts is suggested by the IRS.
- Communicating that the charity will have discretion and control over donor-preferenced gifts is only part of a charity's obligation under the deputized fund-raising concept. Actually demonstrating discretion and control is also a key factor in qualifying a gift as tax-deductible.
- When raising noncompensation project funds, communication with donors should emphasize that funds are being raised for the charity's projects, instead of a missionary's personal projects.
- Charities that utilize deputized fund-raising should carefully establish appropriate policies and procedures and communicate to potential workers who are subject to this concept. Current deputized workers should periodically participate in training to ensure the workers are familiar with the charity's policies.
- When a deputized worker leaves a charity, any balance in the worker's account must remain under the control of the charity and subject to the charity's policies.

Mission agencies and certain other charities often use what is often referred to as a "deputized" fund-raising concept. Deputized fund-raising may also be referred to as "self-supported," "deputational," "individualized," or "staff support-raising."

Under the deputized fund-raising approach, a worker is charged or deputized by the charity with the responsibility to raise gifts to provide sufficient funds to pay part or all of the individual's compensation, fringe benefits, and charity expenses. The charity determines the amount of funds the worker is responsible to raise (both in terms of the compensation the worker will receive and any expenses to be reimbursed to the worker). The concept is an effective alternative to other fund-raising methods because of the greater connection between the donor and self-supported worker.

The term "worker" is used in this book since, in certain instances, the individual may be referred to by the charity as an employee, an independent contractor or a volunteer. Occasionally deputized workers are called volunteers because they have volunteered to serve with a particular organization. However, when "volunteers" are paid amounts reportable on Forms W-2 as employee compensation or on Forms 1099-MISC as nonemployee compensation, the workers have been "paid." Therefore, when workers are "paid," the use of the term "unpaid volunteers" is inaccurate and does not truthfully describe the worker's relationship to the organization in accordance with ECFA's Standard 7.1.

To avoid gifts being treated as nondeductible earmarked gifts (see Chapter 5), contributions to support particular missionaries and other specific workers must qualify as donor-preferenced gifts—preferenced to support the work carried out by a particular individual but not earmarked for the individual (there is a distinction between preferenced and earmarked gifts—for an explanation of preferenced gifts, see pages 15-20).

The deputized fund-raising practice has occasionally drawn the attention of the IRS because of the tendency of some charities to represent that contributions will only be used to support the worker doing the fund-raising. In these instances, the transaction is blurred since donors may be led to believe the organization is merely a conduit for the gifts to the worker.[47]

Types of deputized fund-raising. The two primary deputized fund-raising approaches are often termed the "individual worker" and "pooled" concepts. Under the individual worker approach, the compensation paid to a worker generally bears a direct relationship to the amount raised by the worker, whereas under the pooled approach, compensation is generally paid to the worker without respect to the amount of funds raised by the worker.

The individual worker approach is also often referred to as "deputized" fund-raising as distinguished from "pooled" fund-raising. In reality, under both concepts the worker is charged or deputized with the responsibility to raise funds. Therefore, in this document, both approaches are referred to as "deputized fund-raising," with the "individual worker" and "pooled" methods described as sub-categories under deputized fund-raising.

- **Fund-raising to support the work of individuals.** Funds donated to the charity under this concept are generally recorded in a support account identified for each worker. Charges are made against the support account to fund the individual's compensation, fringe benefits, and other expenses related to the particular sphere of the worker's responsibilities. Charges to cover the organization's overhead are also often made against these support accounts. Compensation to the worker generally bears a relationship to the money raised by that particular worker.

- **Fund-raising to support the work of a group of individuals.** The key to a pooled approach is that funds are raised to support a *group* of workers instead of on a worker-by-worker basis. One example of such a group might be *all* the missionaries relating to a particular organization. Or the group might be a particular team of workers, all of the workers in a country, all of the workers in a group of international fields, or all of the workers in a section of the United States. The grouping may be based on a geographical area, ministry function (for example, evangelistic group vs. the linguistic group), or another grouping that is consistent with the ministry's organizational structure.

  The fund-raising solicitation in the pooled approach must clearly indicate that funds raised for the charity will be used under its control and discretion in support of a project or group of the charity's workers, not for the benefit of an individual worker. For example, the solicitation may identify the geographical area, the team, or other group designation which will benefit from the funds raised.

Although, in a pooled concept, charities often account for donation income on a worker-by-worker basis in order to document each worker's fund-raising accomplishments, the gift income is generally pooled into one temporarily-restricted income account for the entire group. Compensation paid to the worker does not bear a direct relationship to the money that the individual raises. However, compensation could be contingent on funds raised for the entire group.

Under the pooled concept, expenditures are generally tracked by group rather than by supported worker. Balances are not carried forward from one accounting period to the next based on income or expenses relating to a particular worker.

In this concept, the organization predetermines compensation levels for individuals in a group. Pay need not be identical for everyone in a group. But pay is usually based on responsibility, longevity, family size, educational attainment, cost-of-living in a particular country, and a variety of other factors.

The services of workers may be discontinued or redirected based on periodic reviews of the worker's performance. The continuing involvement of a particular worker with an organization could be based, at least in part, on whether the worker is meeting fund-raising goals.

The use of a pooled fund-raising approach seems to demonstrate charity control and discretion, since payments to workers are not based on specific amounts each worker raises. In one significant case, the tax court confirmed tax deductibility of contributions to a ministry utilizing the pooled fund-raising concept. In this case, a donor made gifts to a missionary-sending organization indicating the names of the supported missionaries on the contribution checks.[48] The funds were used by the charity in a shared or pooled support concept.

IRS view of deputized fund-raising. In 1998, an *ad hoc* group led by Milt Cerny, of Caplin & Drysdale, was formed to address deputized fund-raising issues raised by the IRS when it denied the tax-exempt status of an evangelical charity in 1996 and then issued a tax-exemption determination letter to the charity in 1997.[49]

The *ad hoc* group contacted the IRS concerning these issues and the IRS responded with a letter dated May 26, 1999.[50] This letter did not provide adequate guidance, so the *ad hoc* group sought a meeting with the IRS.

In the fall of 1999, Mr. Cerny, George R. "Chip" Grange and Steve King of Gammon and Grange, Lloyd Mayer of Caplin & Drysdale, Forest Montgomery of NAE, and Dan Busby of ECFA, met with David Jones, Chief of the Review Branch, Exempt Organizations, and Mike Finley, Chief of the Branch of the Chief Counsel's Income Tax and Accounting Division with primary responsibility for charitable contribution deduction issues, in the IRS's National Office in Washington, D.C.

Soon after the meeting with IRS officials, the *ad hoc* group drafted a letter to the Section 501(c)(3) tax-exempt staff at the National Office of the IRS. The IRS response to that letter, while nonprecedential, included certain guidelines concerning the demonstration of control and discretion that the IRS believed should be exercised by a charity with respect to gifts raised under the deputized concept.[51] This is the most recent guidance from a high ranking IRS official on this topic.

The IRS acknowledges deputized fund-raising as a widespread and legitimate practice. Contributions properly raised by this method are generally tax-deductible.

In its Technical Instruction Program materials, the IRS outlined two general tests[52] to determine whether a tax-deductible contribution is made to or for the use of a charity, or whether a gift is a non-deductible, pass-through gift to a particular individual who ultimately benefits from the contribution.

- **Intended benefit test.** The purpose of this test is to determine whether the contributor's intent in making the donation is to benefit the charity or an individual.[53] If the donor intends to benefit an individual, there is generally no tax deduction for the gift and the gift should not be accepted by the charity because the gift is not in harmony with the charity's tax-exempt purposes (see Chapter 5).

The IRS provided the following suggested language for use on donor *response documents* to help clarify the true intentions of a donor at the time of the contribution:

> "This contribution is made with the understanding that the donee charity has complete control and administration over the use of the donated funds."

Similarly, the IRS suggests the following language be included in *solicitations* to help show that the charity has the necessary control over contributions and that the charity has adequately communicated to the donor that it has the necessary control and discretion over contributions. This language can be used assuming that there is no conflicting language in other materials or understandings between the parties:

> "Contributions are solicited with the understanding that the donee charity has complete discretion and control over the use of all donated funds."

Use of these statements should provide strong evidence of both donor intent and organizational control in the deputized fund-raising context.

The goal is to communicate to the donor that the gift is only preferenced for the work performed by a particular individual, and it is not restricted only to benefit that individual. To help achieve this mindset in the donor, the following are recommended:

1. There is consistency and clarity in all communications (written, verbal, or through media) including prayer letters, fund-raising letters, and newsletters, clearly reflecting that:

   a. gifts in response to this communication are gifts for the use of the charity. The opportunity to preference the gift to support the ministry of a particular worker is secondary to the identification of the gift for the charity, and,

   b. the particular worker's ministry is being conducted under the direction of the organization.

2. The following statements *should not* be made by the charity or the worker:

   a. "One hundred percent of all contributions designated for Mary Missionary are provided to her." Alternately, an appropriate statement might be: "One hundred percent of all contributions designated for use on the mission field are sent to the mission field." *Note:* The alternate statement is appropriate only if no overhead is charged on these gifts.

   b. "Your gift will be placed into our account and everything in the account is available to us."

   c. "Thank you for your gift to me."

3. Other helpful principles of communication to donors include:

   a. Prayer letters, fund-raising letters, newsletters, and other communications from the worker or the charity to the donor should reference the charity and its work.

   b. Communication by the charity (written, media and verbal) and/or the worker should not refer to gifts to a particular worker, instead they should indicate the gifts are to the charity and are only preferenced for the work of a particular worker.

- **Discretion and control test.** A charity must exercise "discretion and control" over donated funds.[54] Informally, the IRS has stated that discretion and control may be evidenced by such factors as adequate selection and supervision of the supported worker and a formalized budget that establishes the compensation limits for workers and expenses to be paid to or for each deputized individual. Establishing compensation and expense reimbursements with reference to considerations other than the amount of money raised by a deputized worker would demonstrate a charity's discretion and control over funds raised.

  The IRS stated[55] that charities receiving revenues from deputized fund-raising—through individual missionaries, staff members, or volunteers conducting grass-roots fund-raising to support the ministry—can demonstrate discretion and control in the following ways:

1) The charity's governing body (such as the board of directors) exercises control of donated funds through a budgetary process.

2) The governing body consistently establishes, reviews, and monitors the programs and policies of the charity.

3) The charity sets staff salaries, including maximum compensation, according to a salary schedule approved by the governing body. Salaries are set in reference to considerations other than an amount of money a deputized fund-raiser collects. There can be no commitment that contributions will be paid as salary or expenses with respect to a particular person.

4) Amounts paid as salary, to the extent required by the Internal Revenue Code, are reported as compensation.

   Author's note: Deputized workers generally receive Form W-2. Deputized fund-raising guidance from the IRS seems to anticipate the Form W-2 approach, *e.g.,* references to "training, development, and supervision of staff" and "amounts paid as salary." There is one case where the tax court provided an independent contractor determination for a deputized worker.[56] However, the facts in the case do not apply to most deputized workers.

5) Reimbursements of legitimate business expenses are approved by the ministry, pursuant to the governing body's guidelines. Reimbursements must be set by considerations other than the amount of money a deputized fund-raiser collects.

6) Potential staff members are thoroughly screened according to qualifications established by the charity. These are related to the charity's exempt purposes and not principally related to the amount of funds the staff members may raise.

7) Staff members are given meaningful training, development, and supervision.

Gifts to Support Deputized Workers

Type of Gift	Complies with ECFA Standards	Qualifies as a Charitable Deduction for Donor
Personal gifts from an individual to a deputized worker [(1)] [(2)]	Not applicable	No
Payment[(3)] from a charity to/for a deputized worker – not based on gifts restricted or preferenced by a donor(s)	Yes	Yes
Payment[(3)] from a charity to/for a deputized worker based on gifts preferenced for a particular deputized worker. The donor's intent is to benefit the charity.	Yes	Generally acceptable
Payment[(3)] from a charity to/for a deputized worker based on gifts restricted or preferenced for a particular deputized worker. The donor's intent is to benefit a particular deputized worker.	No – Intent of donor must be to benefit the charity	Generally, no. Intent of donor must be to benefit the charity

(1) Personal gifts from an individual to a deputized worker may have estate tax implications if the gifts to a particular individual exceed the annual gift tax limitation.

(2) In some instances, the IRS has taken the position that a gift from an individual to a deputized worker is taxable income to the worker if the worker is not a family member of the donor.

(3) Payment representing compensation, fringe benefits, reimbursement of business expenses

8) The charity assigns staff members to programs and project locations based upon its assessment of each staff member's skills and training and the specific needs of the ministry.

9) Regular communication through such means as newsletters, solicitation literature, and donor receipts informing donors of the charity's full control and discretion over its programs and funds.

10) The charity's financial policies and practices are annually reviewed by the board or an audit committee, a majority of whose members are independent.

Clear communication with donors about the discretion and control issue not only places donors on notice, it serves to reinforce this concept in the mind of the deputized worker. Too often, workers raising funds under the deputized concept assume an element of personal ownership over the funds they raise for the ministry.

Example 1: When worker A leaves the employment of charity B, the worker may mistakenly believe that the balance in his or her account should be transferred to charity C (worker A's new employer), where the worker will be employed. While a transfer to charity C may be made if it furthers the charitable purpose of charity B, it is not required.

Example 2: When worker D leaves the employment of charity E after completing a two-year missionary term, there is a substantial excess of funds raised for the charity by worker D above what was spent for the ministry of this worker. The worker may mistakenly believe the excess in his or her account should be paid to the worker. While a modest severance payment might be made to the worker in conformity with the charity's policies, the excess is an asset of the charity and subject to the charity's discretion and control.

Developing policies and communicating them to workers. Charities that utilize deputized fund-raising should carefully establish appropriate policies and procedures (see sample policy on pages 145-47). Once the policies are created, they should be included in a training manual to explain the process of deputized fund-raising to potential workers. The training manual should be annually distributed and updated for all current and potential deputized workers. Training classes should also be utilized to educate new and potential deputized workers about their support-raising activities. Current deputized workers should periodically participate in ongoing training to ensure the workers are familiar with the charity's policies.

Communicating a charity's policies to donors. It is important that charities determine how to notify their donors that they will exercise discretion and control over the donations. The best way to inform donors of deputized fund-raising policies, and consequently the ministry's control and discretion, is to use the IRS recommended language in written and verbal solicitations and response documents. The following is an example of wording for communicating ministry discretion and control to donors:

> Contributions are solicited with the understanding that ABC Missionary Agency has complete discretion and control over the use of all donated funds. The charity will attempt to honor gifts preferenced to support particular workers but the final decision on the use of all funds rests with the charity.

It is important that charities who utilize deputized fund-raising ensure its compliance with ministry-established policies and procedures. Financial policies and control practices should be periodically reviewed to assure that control elements outlined in the organization's policy do exist and are well documented. Among these controls should be the approval of work-related expenses, approval of general and overhead allocations, and the ability to redirect funds within the charity's operation in the event a worker is terminated or the worker's ministry changes.

Communication by deputized workers to prospective donors. It is important that a charity utilize consistent communications with its donors. Careful review of current documents, such as solicitation letters (including "prayer" letters), emails, donor response forms, deputized worker training materials, gift acknowledgments, gift response forms, and other related documents will help eliminate conflicts or contradictions. It is also important to establish procedures to ensure that such reviews are ongoing.

Appropriate terminology should always be used when communicating with donors. Since the ministry should not commit contributions (to be paid as salary or to reimburse expenses) to a particular person, deputized fund-raisers should never imply they would be, verbally or in writing. A donor may indicate a preference that the charity use a gift to support the ministry of a certain individual and the charity may track the dollars based on that preference. But the charity and the deputized worker should refrain from any inference that the contributions or a percentage of it will be paid as salary or expense reimbursements to the worker (see pages 139-44 for sample deputized fund-raising letters to a prospective donor and related response forms).

Requesting donations preferenced for a particular worker related to noncompensation costs. Occasionally, workers desire to raise funds for specific travel expenses, specific projects, medical expenses, education expenses of their children, a personally-owned auto, adoption expenses and more. Technical guidance in this area is scant.

The following guidelines may be helpful in addressing these types of specific funding requests:

1. All funds raised by workers under the deputized fund-raising concept are to accomplish the charitable purposes of the charity. The workers are only representatives of the charity.

2. If a charity determines that a project accomplishes its charitable purposes (charitable purposes do not include personal purposes), the organization could delegate the fund-raising for the project to a specific worker. The fact that the worker initially suggested the idea for the project should not diminish the project's worthiness if the charity approved the project before the worker communicated the giving opportunity to donors.

   A key element in communicating project needs by a charity or a worker is clarifying that funds are being raised for the charity's projects instead of a missionary's personal projects. Here are two examples of communication with donors:

Example 1: "I want to share an exciting opportunity with you. I am building a church in XYZ province. I need $25,000 for this project. Please make your checks payable to ABC Mission for this project."

This fund-raising communication is problematic because the project description implies this is a personal project instead of ABC Mission's project. Thus, the tax-deductibility of gifts is likely at risk.

Example 2: "ABC Mission has approved the building of a church in XYZ province at a projected cost of $25,000. This church will significantly complement the ministry of ABC Mission in the province where I have ministered for the last three years. Will you partner with ABC Mission in building this church and provide your check payable to ABC?"

The wording of this example clearly demonstrates that gifts are to the charity and for the ministry of the charity. The fact that the worker is the one who initiated the request for the church in this province is irrelevant.

3. Could a missionary-sending charity temporarily raise the compensation limit for a particular missionary couple needing a lump-sum to adopt a child or purchase a car, for example, so they could receive extra amounts to cover the expenses (and the missionary couple asks supporters for funds to cover the adoption expenses or car within the higher compensation limit)? Since child adoption and the purchase of a personal car are not business expenses, this approach may be very questionable. However, soliciting more funds to accommodate financial needs in general is often reasonable if the higher compensation does not result in excess benefit to the worker; *e.g.,* the worker is not paid more than is justified under a performance-based compensation approach.

Organizations which may not provide adequate oversight for missionaries. Certain organizations only provide minimal oversight in relation to workers receiving funds from the organization. Some of these organizations provide a service that basically amounts to providing receipts to donors and passing the money along to the workers.

The following are some characteristics often attributed to charities that provide a "servicing" program for individual workers:

- The servicing charity accepts gifts earmarked for specific workers and passes through all funds received less a modest service charge, such as three to five percent.
- The servicing charity provides little, if any, administrative oversight over the workers serviced.
- Workers are free to raise as much money as they can.
- Workers serviced do not regularly report their ministry activities to the servicing charity.
- Workers are not required to meet any qualifications before participating with the charity.

Even though a servicing entity may have tax-exempt status from the IRS, if the organization were scrutinized by the IRS, it is possible that:

1. gifts handled by the organization might be termed earmarked and thus not qualify as charitable deductions, and
2. the leaders of the organization might be subject to potential intermediate sanctions or the IRS might revoke the organization's tax-exempt status.

Sequencing of payments to deputized workers. It is important that compensation be paid before expenses are reimbursed. If expenses are reimbursed before compensation, the arrangement is a nonaccountable reimbursement plan and all expense reimbursements are taxable as compensation.[57]

> ***Example:*** An organization establishes an account on January 1 for a worker who raises funds under the deputized concept. The monthly salary of the worker is established as $1,800. In January, $2,000 worth of gifts are received as preferenced for the worker and posted to an account preferenced for the

support of this worker. The expenses for this worker for January are $600.

Option A: The organization pays $1,800 to the worker as compensation for January, $200 for expenses and tracks the $400 of unpaid expenses. The $200 expense reimbursement is tax-free if reimbursed under an accountable plan.

Option B: The organization pays $600 of expenses and $1,400 of compensation for January. The $600 expense reimbursement is fully taxable since the entire monthly compensation was not paid before the expense reimbursements.

Donor-restricted scholarships for deputized workers. Gifts that are restricted for scholarships for deputized workers are subject to much more stringent rules than for gifts preferenced for the support of a deputized worker. For example, a donor preferencing a gift for the support of a worker under the deputized fund-raising concept generally knows the identity of the worker before the gift is made. In contrast, the knowledge by the donor of the recipient of a scholarship would create substantial risk that the contribution would not qualify for a charitable gift deduction.[58] Therefore, a scholarship for deputized workers should be treated as compensation to the deputized worker unless the scholarship is used to reimburse education expense that qualifies for reimbursement by the charity as an education expense.

Separation from service. When a deputized worker leaves a charity, any balance in the worker's account must remain under the control of the charity. Policies of the charity may provide that such balances may be redirected by the charity to a second charity with a similar mission statement and for a similar purpose. These policy statements should be communicated to the worker before or at the time the person begins service with the organization and on or near the date of his or her service separation.

When a worker separates from service, donors who have been making gifts to the charity preferenced for the support of the worker should be notified immediately, allowing those donors to decide if they wish to continue to support the charity.

Organizations sometimes establish policies which allow payments for a reasonable time period after the severance date, such as two to four months. The severance payments are typically limited to the amount of funds raised.

Payments to a retired deputized worker or spouse. Raising funds to supplement the retirement income for missionaries is sometimes done. This concept is generally more acceptable if the funds are raised for a retiree pool rather than missionary-by-missionary. The pooling of funds for retirement payments provides better evidence of a charity's control over the funds. It is difficult to justify payments to the spouse of a deceased missionary if the spouse was not a recipient of compensation (Form W-2 or Form 1099-MISC) during the years of active service with the charity.

Mission organizations that are not churches are subject to ERISA, which generally prohibits vague, unfunded, undefined retirement programs. Mission organizations that are churches are generally prohibited from using retirement programs unless they are qualified plans or they are specifically documented in such a way that a benefit will only be paid when it is due under the plan.[59]

Gifts preferenced for non-U.S. workers. The guidelines in this publication pertaining to deputized workers equally applies to non-U.S. workers. The discretion and control that must be exercised over U.S. citizens working with a U.S. charity must also be exercised with respect to funds that are preferenced for a foreign national. If the discretion and control factors are present for a foreign national, gifts preferenced for the ministry of the foreign national should qualify as a charitable contribution. Charities should exercise care to assure compliance with tax and immigration laws for any national worker that does fund-raising while visiting the U.S. Charities should also take reasonable steps to ensure funds do not go to individuals on the Treasury Department's Specially Designated Nationals (SDN) list or other terrorist and international criminal lists.

Chapter Review 7

1. Is deputized fund-raising a recognized and legitimate practice in which charities and donors may participate? Yes. The IRS acknowledges deputized fund-raising as a widespread and legitimate practice. Contributions properly raised under this method are generally tax-deductible.

2. Has the IRS provided well-defined guidance for the concept of raising funds under the deputized concept? No. The de facto standards in this area are based on a combination of tax law, court rulings and nonprecedential communication from the IRS.

3. Is there more than one type of deputized fund-raising? Yes. The most common type of deputized fund-raising is to support an individual's work. Under another concept, funds may be raised to support the work of a group of individuals.

4. How and when does a charity communicate its discretion and control over a gift raised on the deputized fund-raising basis? Charities should communicate to donors, verbally and/or in writing, before and after a gift is made under the deputized fund-raising concept.

5. If the donor intends to benefit an individual instead of a charity, does the gift meet the deputized fund-raising guidelines? No. If a donor intends to benefit an individual, the gift is generally termed "earmarked" and should not be accepted by the charity because the gift is not in harmony with the charity's tax-exempt purposes (see Chapter 5).

6. What steps should a charity take if it has accepted an earmarked gift? First, consider whether a refund of the amount to the donor is appropriate. Second, do not issue a charitable gift acknowledgment. Finally, for accounting purposes, record the amount as an agency transaction (as a liability on the Statement of Financial Position).

7. How does a charity demonstrate discretion and control with respect to gifts raised under the deputized concept? Discretion and control is generally evidenced by such factors as adequate selection and supervision of workers and a formalized budget that establishes compensation limits for workers and expenses to be paid to or for each deputized individual. The IRS has suggested 10 specific guidelines for a charity to follow in demonstrating discretion and control.

8. Is it important for a charity to have policies outlining its discretion and control over gifts and to communicate the policies to deputized workers? Yes. Before a deputized worker begins to raise funds for a charity, the worker should receive a copy of the charity's policies with respect to the charity's control over deputized gifts. Current deputized workers should periodically participate in on-going training to ensure the worker is familiar with the charity's policies.

9. Is it appropriate for workers to raise funds specifically for personal purposes (such as for an auto or a home that will be personally owned)? Generally, no, because an organization's charitable purposes do not include funding a worker's personal expenses.

10. Is it appropriate to reimburse a deputized worker's expenses before disbursing compensation to the worker? No. This practice is a nonaccountable reimbursement plan and all expense reimbursements are taxable as compensation.

11. When a deputized worker separates from service with the charity, is it appropriate for the charity to pay the worker a sum equal to the balance in the worker's account? Generally, no, unless the payments are in compliance with the charity's severance policy.

12. When a deputized worker separates from service with a charity and begins to work for another charity, should the first charity disburse the funds in the worker's account to the second charity? When a deputized worker leaves a charity, any balance in the worker's account must remain under the control of the charity. Policies of the charity may provide that such balances may be redirected by the charity to a second charity with a similar mission statement for a similar purpose.

Chapter 8

Contributions to Support Short-Term Mission Trips

Executive Summary

- Participants in short-term mission trips are often responsible to raise part or all of the expenses relating to the trip.
- As with the deputized fund-raising concept (see Chapter 7), the donor's intent must be to benefit the charity rather than an individual.
- The charity is responsible to demonstrate discretion and control over gifts given for short-term mission trips.
- If a charity sponsors a mission trip which is not for pleasure or personal gain, gifts for it are generally tax deductible, even if given by a trip participant.
- The sponsoring charity should follow a policy of not refunding gifts when intended trip participants do not go on the trip. Refunding gifts for short-term mission trips may jeopardize the tax-deductibility of all amounts paid for the charity's mission trips.
- In the accounting records, gifts for trip participants should be recorded as charitable gifts, not as a liability until the trip is completed.
- Charities that conduct short-term mission trips and charge a fee to intermediary charities for trip participants, such as churches, should generally record the amounts received as fee revenue even though the payments by trip participants and their sponsors to the intermediary charity may qualify as charitable contributions.

Many churches and parachurch organizations sponsor individuals and/or teams of individuals that serve on short-term mission trips, domestically and internationally. The proper handling of funds raised and expended for short-term mission trips often raises some challenging issues (accounting issues are addressed on pages 119-20).

The definition of "short-term" varies from one sponsoring organization to another. For church-sponsored trips, a short-term mission trip often means a trip of a week or two in duration. However, for a missions organization, a short-term trip may last as long as two years. Short-term mission trips sometimes only involve adults. Other times, participants are minors, supervised by adults, or some combination of adults and minors.

Funding options for short-term mission trips. Short-term mission trips may be funded in a variety of ways. For example, the sponsoring organization may pay part or all of the expenses of the trip from the organization's general budget. Or a donor may give funds restricted for short-term mission trips without any preference or reference as to particular mission trip participants—the donor simply wishes to support the program of sending short-term missionaries. However, most organizations sponsoring short-term mission trips seek gifts that are preferenced for particular trip participants.

- **Funding from the sponsoring organization's general budget.** Expenses relating to short-term mission trips may be funded in full by the sponsoring organization, a church or parachurch organization. The use of funds from the general budget of a nonprofit organization is appropriate if short-term mission trips are consistent with the tax-exempt purposes of the sponsoring charity.

- **Funds directly expended by the trip participant with no financial involvement of the sponsoring organization.** A participant in a short-term mission trip may partially or totally fund trip expenses by making direct payments for airfare, lodging, meals, and other expenses. If a trip is sponsored or approved by a charity, the trip is consistent with the tax-exempt purposes of the charity, and there is no significant element of personal pleasure, recreation or vacation,[60] expenses related to the trip are generally deductible as charitable contributions on the taxpayer's Schedule A.

Personal expenses relating to "side-trips" or vacation days included in the trip are generally not deductible.

A taxpayer can claim a charitable contribution deduction for travel expenses necessarily incurred while away from home performing services for a charitable organization only if there is no significant element of personal pleasure, recreation, or vacation in such travel. This applies whether a taxpayer pays the expenses directly or indirectly. Expenses are paid indirectly if a taxpayer makes a payment to the charitable organization and the organization pays the travel expenses. The deduction will not be denied simply because the taxpayer enjoys providing services to the charitable organization.[61]

If a donor makes a single contribution of $250 or more in paying short-term mission trip expenses, the donor must have—and the charity should provide—a written acknowledgment (see example on page 155). The acknowledgment must include:

1. A description of the services provided by the donor (such as built church building, shared the gospel on the beach);
2. A statement of whether or not the sponsoring organization provided the donor with any goods or services to reimburse the donor for the expenses incurred;
3. A description and a good faith estimate of the value of any goods or services (other than intangible religious benefits) provided to reimburse the donor; and
4. A statement of any intangible religious benefits provided to the donor.

- **Funding based on donor-restricted gifts for the trip but with no preference in relation to any trip participant.** Donors may make gifts restricted for a short-term mission trip project or fund. Gifts for the project could be solicited by the charity or the donor might make an unsolicited gift. These gifts generally qualified as charitable contributions and it is appropriate for the sponsoring charity to provide a charitable gift acknowledgment.

  If a charity accepts gifts that are donor-restricted for a short-term mission trip project or fund, the charity is obligated to spend the funds for the intended purpose. The only exceptions are generally if the donor releases the restriction, excess funds are carried over for future trips, or if the excess funds are minimal.

- **Funding based on gifts preferenced for particular trip participants.** Mission trip participants generally are responsible for soliciting gifts to cover part or all of the expenses necessary for the particular trip (see pages 151-52 for a sample letter from a potential short-term mission trip participant to a potential donor).

  When mission trip participants raise part or all of the funds required for a trip, the sponsoring organization generally records the amounts raised in separate accounts for each participant as a way of monitoring whether sufficient funds have been raised to cover the expenses of each individual's trip. Charges are then made against the particular account for expenses incurred for the trip. Occasionally, charges will be made to the accounts for the particular short-term mission trip participants in relation to the charity's overhead expenses for the trip.

  Gifts preferenced for particular trip participants should not be refunded to donors if the preferenced individual does not go on the trip. Refunding these gifts is a strong indication that the sponsoring charity does not have adequate discretion and control over the gifts and the issue of earmarked gifts is raised.

  When funds are raised for a short-term mission trip on a participant-by-participant basis, the deputized fund-raising guidelines generally apply (see Chapter 7). When a worker or a volunteer (a short-term mission trip participant typically fits the definition of a "volunteer") raises some of his or her own support, the IRS has proposed the following two general tests to determine whether a tax-deductible contribution was made to or for the use of a charitable organization, or whether the gift was a nondeductible, pass-through gift to a particular individual who ultimately benefited from the contribution.

  1. **The intended benefit test.** The purpose of this test is to determine whether the contributor's intent in making the donation was to benefit the organization or the individual.

The IRS has formally indicated that organizations are to avoid the use of conflicting language in their solicitations for contributions, and to avoid conflicts in understandings between the parties. This is to demonstrate that the:

a. qualified donee has exercised the necessary control over contributions;

b. donor has reason to know that the qualified donee will have the necessary discretion and control over contributions; and

c. donor intends for the qualified donee to be the actual recipient of the contributions.

The following statement should be used in solicitations for contributions:

> *Contributions are solicited with the understanding that the donee organization has complete discretion and control over the use of all donated funds.*

2. **The discretion and control test.** The IRS uses the phrase "discretion and control" to indicate a charity's obligation regarding deputized funds. The IRS stated that charities receiving revenues from fund-raising for the support of career or short-term mission endeavors can demonstrate control and discretion with the following directives:

   a. Reimbursement of legitimate ministry expenses are approved by the organization, pursuant to the governing body's guidelines. Reimbursement must be set by considerations other than the amount of money collected by the individuals who raise funds.

   b. Potential trip members are screened according to qualifications established by the organization.

   c. Trip members are given meaningful training, development, and supervision.

   d. The organization assigns trip members to programs and project locations based upon its assessment of each individual's skills and training, and the specific needs of the organization.

e. Donor receipts inform donors of the organization's full control and discretion over its programs and funds.

f. Since the organization should not commit contributions to a particular person, potential trip participants should never imply the opposite, verbally or in writing. A donor may indicate a preference that the charity use a gift to support the trip of a certain individual, and the charity may track the dollars based on that preference. However, the organization and the potential trip participant should refrain from any inference that the contributions will be paid as expenses to or for a particular worker. This is a fine line, but one that should be carefully observed.

Assuming the intended benefit and control tests are met, the tax deductibility issues of contributions for short-term mission trips are based on age, charity authorization, and the pursuit of pleasure or personal gain. Two potentially tax-deductible scenarios follow:

Example 1: **The trip participants are adults.**

a. Participants contribute to the charity to cover the entire amount of the trip expenses. The payments by the participants to the charity are deductible as charitable contributions if the trip involves no significant element of personal pleasure, recreation, or vacation. These trip contributions may be receipted by the charity as charitable contributions.

b. All trip expenses are paid by the charity, and non-participants make contributions to cover trip expenses of participants who cannot afford to pay all of their own expenses. If the charity has preauthorized the mission trip, the trip furthers the exempt purposes of the charity, and if the trip involves no significant element of personal pleasure, recreation, or vacation, gifts to cover the travel expenses of participants who cannot afford to pay all travel expenses are generally tax deductible, even if the donors indicate a preference that gifts be applied to the trip expenses of a particular participant.

Example 2: **Trip participants are minors.** If a trip participant is a minor, the minor must actually provide services to carry out the tax-exempt purposes of the trip. The age of the minor and the minor's development may be important factors in determining the minor's capability of providing services to the charity.

If parents, relatives, and/or friends contribute to the charity with a preference for their children's trip expenses, and the charity pays the trip expenses, these contributions are generally tax deductible (assuming the minor significantly contributes to the charity's trip purposes).[62]

- **Funding based on gifts restricted for particular trip participants.** Although a donor may express a *preference* for a particular trip recipient, if a donor expresses a *restriction* for a certain trip recipient, the gift may be considered earmarked. Therefore, the gift may not qualify for a charitable deduction and should generally not be accepted (or acknowledged as a gift if accepted) by a charity sponsoring a short-term mission trip.

  An earmarked gift is a transfer that is intended to benefit an individual, not the charity. It is a transfer over which the charity does not have sufficient discretion and control. In the short-term mission trip context, if the charity accepted a gift restricted for a particular trip participant, the charity would not have the freedom to use the funds for a trip participant who fell short of the financial goal for the trip.

  Sponsors of short-term mission trips generally should not accept gifts earmarked for individuals because the gifts are not consistent with the charity's tax-exempt purposes.

Chapter Review 8

1. Are gifts to support short-term mission trips deductible as charitable gifts? Generally, yes, but it depends on the facts and circumstances. To be tax-deductible, gifts to support a trip participant, especially gifts from the trip participant, must be subject to the discretion and control of the sponsoring charity, the trip must be for legitimate mission purposes, and the trip participants must fulfill those purposes.

2. Is it appropriate for a charity to sponsor and fund a short-term mission trip with funds in the charity's budget or with funds raised for a short-term mission trip project (its donors did not indicate an interest in supporting any particular participant)? Yes, if the purposes of the trip are consistent with the tax-exempt purposes of the charity and there is no significant element of personal pleasure, recreation or vacation with respect to the participants.

3. Can short-term mission trip participants pay part or all of the trip expenses out of their pocket, with no financial involvement of the sponsoring charity? Yes, if the trip is sponsored or approved by the charity, the trip is consistent with the tax-exempt purposes of the charity and there is no significant element of personal pleasure, recreation or vacation. If the trip meets these thresholds, the charity should provide a written acknowledgment to the trip participant for out-of-pocket expenses.

4. Is it appropriate for a donor to indicate a preference or express a desire that a gift be used to fund the trip of a particular participant, even if the donor is the trip participant or a relative? If only a preference is made for the gift to be used to fund the expenses of a particular participant, and refunds are not given to prospective participants who are not able to go on the trip, gifts are generally deductible if the trip is sponsored or approved by the charity, the trip is consistent with the tax-exempt purposes of the charity and there is no significant element of personal pleasure, recreation or vacation.

5. Are funds given to a charity deductible when the gifts are preferenced for particular trip participants and the participants are minors? It depends. The minor must actually provide services to carry out the tax-exempt purposes of the trip. The age of the minor and minor's development may be important factors in determining the minor's capability of providing services to the charity.

6. Should funds ever be refunded to donors when a potential short-term missions trip participant does not go on the trip and gifts have been preferenced for that individual? Generally, no. Sponsoring charities should have a policy prohibiting refunds of gifts relating to short-term mission trips. Refunding a mission trip gift shows lack of the necessary discretion and control by the sponsoring charity over gifts, thereby placing the tax-deductibility of the gifts at risk.

Chapter 9

Accounting Issues

Executive Summary

- For accounting purposes, restricted gifts must be identified either as permanently restricted, where the principal must remain intact in perpetuity, or as temporarily restricted based on purpose or time restrictions.
- Temporarily-restricted revenue should be recorded separately from unrestricted revenue. This provides the basis for determining when donor restrictions have been satisfied.
- Most states have adopted a "total return" concept, permitting charities to treat capital appreciation on restricted funds as unrestricted or temporarily-restricted income if the charity's board determines this treatment is prudent.
- Gifts that support the charity's programs preferenced for specific workers should be treated as revenues and expenses of the charity. The gift preferencing does not restrict the gift. However, other gift limitations may result in a restricted gift.
- Although charities should generally turn down earmarked gifts (see Chapter 5), if accepted they typically should not be reflected in revenues and expenses but treated as agency transactions.
- Unconditional promises to give should be recorded as revenue at fair value at the time the pledge is received by the charity. "Faith promises" are generally considered conditional promises and not recorded in the accounting records until the gift is collected.
- Gifts to a charity preferenced for a particular worker are generally temporarily-restricted revenue. The gift preferencing does not create a restriction. However, the specific activity in which the worker is engaged is generally the basis of the restriction.

Caring for the intricacies of tax law is only part of the equation for donor-restricted gifts. Accounting principles must be applied to restricted gifts so the contributions will be properly receipted and recorded as temporarily- or permanently-restricted revenue and net assets in the accounting records.

1. **Permanently restricted.** Some donor restrictions permanently limit the organization's use of the contributed asset. For example, gifts of cash and securities that must be invested in perpetuity to provide the organization with an ongoing source of income are permanently restricted.

   If an organization receives a permanently-restricted contribution, it must identify those assets separately from other operating assets. Permanently-restricted contributions are commonly referred to as endowments, where the organization may spend the earnings but may not spend any of the principal. The principal must remain intact in perpetuity. There are some endowments that are not permanently restricted, such as an endowment created for a term of years—a temporarily-restricted endowment—or created by the designation of certain unrestricted net assets by a charity's board (a quasi-endowment).

2. **Temporarily restricted.** Contributions with temporary donor-imposed restrictions limit the use of the gifts to later periods or later specific dates (referred to as time restrictions), specific purposes (referred to as purpose restrictions), or both. Temporary donor restrictions expire either by passage of time or as a result of actions taken by the organization.

   Normally, only the use of related net assets are restricted, not the specific assets. (For example, unless a donor otherwise restricts, donee organizations have the power to exchange assets given to fund a restricted gift; *e.g.,* a gift of stock or land is sold and the proceeds are reinvested.)

Examples of contributions with purpose or time restrictions are as follows:

- A contribution raised to support a particular program by an organization that has multiple programs is an example of a contribution with a temporary purpose restriction.

- Cash received in connection with a campaign to raise funds for renovating a facility would be reported as temporarily-restricted contribution revenue until the purpose restriction was met.

- A charitable reminder unitrust is an example of a gift that has a time restriction—the assets cannot be used until the termination of the trust, normally at the death of the specified beneficiary.

- Contributions of long-lived assets (such as equipment or buildings) that, by their nature, are used up over time, should be recognized as temporarily-restricted gifts if the donor stipulates a period over which the asset must be used by the charity.

- Contributions of unconditional promises to give with payments due in future periods are implicitly temporarily-restricted gifts unless the donor expressly stipulates, or circumstances surrounding the receipt of the promise make clear, that the gift is intended to be used to support activities of the current period.

Key financial statement reporting principles. The fundamental financial statement reporting principles related to donor-restricted gifts includes the following:

- **Board designations of unrestricted net assets.** Board designations may be segregated and displayed separately within the unrestricted class, if desired, but board designations do not create restrictions on otherwise unrestricted net assets.

- **Restricted net assets balances.** It is not possible to release more restricted amounts than a charity started with. Any "overspending" of restricted net assets should be charged to the unrestricted class, unless there is an unconditional pledge to cover the deficit, in which case, recording the pledge will cause the temporarily-restricted class to show at least a break-even balance.

- **Contributions revenue related to pledges receivable.** Contribution revenue related to pledges receivable should generally be reflected as temporarily restricted because of the implied time restriction, unless (a) the donor has stipulated that when the pledge is paid, the gift is permanently restricted, in which case the revenue is initially recorded directly in that class, or (b) explicit donor stipulations or other circumstances surrounding the receipt of the promise make it clear that the donor's intention is to support activities of the current period.

- **Reporting restricted expenses.** All expenses should be reported as decreases in unrestricted net assets. Losses may be reported in any class.

- **Temporarily-restricted contribution revenue.** In some situations, an organization may meet the donor-imposed restrictions on all or a portion of the amount contributed in the same reporting period in which the contribution is received (see "Satisfaction of Donor Restrictions" on pages 111-13).

- **Disclosing the nature of restrictions.** The nature of restrictions on both temporarily- and permanently-restricted net assets should be disclosed in the footnotes to the financial statements.

- **Reclassifications or transfers.** Reclassifications or transfers should not be made *out of* permanently restricted or *into* temporarily or permanently restricted with the following exceptions:

  1. Reclassification is permitted for the matching portion of a restricted matching gift or grant.

  2. Reclassification is permitted if the donor of a gift changes the nature of a restriction in an accounting year subsequent to initial recording of the gift.[63]

- **Restatements of prior-period financial statements.** The terms "restatement" and "reclassification" are often confused. Any error in the financial statements of a prior period discovered subsequent to their issuance should be reported as a prior-period adjustment by restating (a restatement) the prior-period financial statements. A reclassification is a simultaneous increase in one net asset class (such as unrestricted net assets) and a decrease in another (such as temporarily restricted net assets). See the Glossary for further explanation of reclassifications.

Recording donor-restricted gifts in the accounting records. Even if it appears temporarily-restricted gifts meet the criteria (see pages 111-13) for reporting as unrestricted support, it is wise to record the gifts as temporarily restricted. If a charity records donor-restricted gifts as unrestricted on the assumption that the donor's restrictions will be satisfied within the accounting period and then the restrictions are not satisfied, it may be challenging to make the necessary reclassification entries. For example, in January, a calendar-year charity distributes a fund-raising appeal for a specific project. Donor-restricted gifts are received during January-March in response to the appeal. The charity could take two approaches with respect to these gifts: one proper and one improper.

- **Proper process.** Record the gifts as temporarily-restricted revenue. Assign a code to the appeal to record the corresponding revenue and assign a related expense account. In this way, the funds received in response to the appeal and the related expenses will be properly reflected. If the criteria are met to reflect the data as unrestricted activity, a charity will have the information to accommodate this recording of the data. If the criteria are not met, the appropriate reflection of temporarily-restricted activity is shown.

- **Improper process.** All the funds received for the project were not expended within the accounting period. However, at the time the gifts were solicited and received, the charity believed all of the funds raised for the project would be expended within the current accounting year (by December 31). Therefore, the charity did not track the donations for the project in the donor accounting system and recorded all of the gifts as unrestricted. Similarly, expenses for the project were not separately tracked.

  At the end of the accounting period, the charity may not have adequate revenue and expense information with respect to the project to properly reflect the data on the financial statements.

Satisfaction of donor restrictions. Restricted gifts are recognized as income when received or unconditionally promised unless an organization is able to fully satisfy a donor's restrictions in the same period the contribution is received. When that happens, the restricted contribution may be reported immediately as unrestricted support if the organization:

- applies the policy to all donor-restricted gifts,
- has a similar policy for reporting investment gains and income,

- applies the policy consistently from period to period, and
- discloses the policy in the notes to the financial statements.[64]

Although the reporting exception as described above is permitted, reporting all temporarily-restricted contributions as temporarily restricted for audit purposes and reclassifying the portion for which donor restrictions have been satisfied is generally recommended for the following reasons:

- It is generally more consistent with the way funds have been raised.
- Donors often anticipate seeing donor-restricted contributions reflected as temporarily-restricted revenue and reclassified when donor restrictions are satisfied.
- While the exception above might be applied to activities and projects of very short duration (started and completed in the same fiscal period), using this exception to record significant amounts of temporarily-restricted revenue (and only showing the unspent balance at the end of the fiscal period as temporarily-restricted revenue) does not seem to be a beneficial approach with respect to readers of the financial statements.

Under certain circumstances, a charity may reclassify temporarily-restricted net assets to unrestricted as depreciation of long-lived assets is recognized. This reclassification method may be used when:

- A charity has received contributions of long-lived assets (such as property and equipment) or of cash and other assets restricted to the purchase of long-lived assets, for which donors have not expressly stipulated how or how long the long-lived asset must be used by the organization or how to use any proceeds resulting from the asset's disposal.
- The charity has adopted an accounting policy of applying time restrictions on the use of such contributed assets that expire over the assets' expected useful lives, and follows it consistently for all such assets.[65]

When this method is followed, the contributions received should be reported as restricted support that increases temporarily-restricted net assets. Depreciation should be recorded over the asset's useful life, and net assets should be reclassified periodically from temporarily restricted to unrestricted as depreciation is recognized.[66]

In the year that a change is made to reclassify temporarily-restricted net assets to unrestricted as depreciation of long-lived assets is recognized, a footnote might be included in the financial statements such as:

> In accordance with the reporting provision of Statement on Financial Accounting Standards (SFAS) No. 116, paragraph 168, a change in the method of accounting for the release of restrictions for capital assets is made to recognize the release of the restriction over the same period that the related asset is being depreciated in order to better match revenues and expenses. Previously, the restriction was released in full in the year in which the capital asset was acquired or construction was completed. A one-time adjustment is required in the year that the change is made.

Subsequent to the year in which the change in accounting method is made, the following footnote might be included in the financial statements:

> In accordance with the reporting provision of SFAS No. 116, paragraph 168, the release of restrictions for capital assets is recognized over the same period that the related asset is being depreciated.

Donor restrictions on otherwise unrestricted net assets. It is possible for donors to impose restrictions on otherwise unrestricted net assets, as well as on their own contributions. A donor may make a restricted contribution that is conditioned on the charity restricting a certain amount of its unrestricted net assets. If the charity accepts the gift, the restrictions are not reversible without the donor's consent and result in a reclassification of unrestricted net assets to temporarily- or permanently-restricted net assets.[67]

> ***Example:*** Larry Bonds made a contribution of $200,000 to the North Central Seminary to establish a permanent endowment with the stipulation that the seminary match the contribution with $100,000 of

> unrestricted net assets. If the seminary accepts the donation, $100,000 of unrestricted net assets would be reclassified to permanently-restricted net assets and the seminary would have no discretion to release those permanent restrictions.

If a charity allows donors to place restrictions on previously unrestricted net assets, the charity should consider whether it is desirable to explain the reclassification of unrestricted net assets in a note to the financial statements. (Financial statement users expect to see reclassifications from temporarily-restricted net assets to unrestricted net assets, but a reverse transfer of net assets might be difficult to understand unless it is explained in a note to the financial statements.)

In such a case, when a donor places a restriction on previously unrestricted net assets, a sample financial statement disclosure may be as follows:

> Note 6 – Reclassification of Net Assets
>
> During 2008, the seminary received a $200,000 contribution to its permanent endowment fund conditioned upon the seminary matching the amount with $100,000 of unrestricted funds, which also must be retained permanently at the donor's request. As a result of this contribution, the seminary's financial statements reflect a $100,000 reclassification of unrestricted net assets to permanently-restricted net assets.

Returning restricted contributions. A charity may be required to return a contribution if it is unable to comply with donor restrictions, or the charity has received a court order requiring it to return the contribution (see pages 45-46). A charity may also choose to return a contribution if the donor has changed his or her mind about giving to the charity. If a charity returns a restricted donation received in a prior year, a loss should generally be recorded since expenses are not be reported in the restricted net asset classes. If a restricted contribution received in the current year is returned, the charity could decrease contribution revenue instead of recording a loss.

The return of a donation may have income tax return filing implications for the donor. See pages 155-56 for sample letters to the donor.

Donor restrictions imposed after the date of the gift. Occasionally, a donor makes a contribution but reserves the right to specify the purpose of the gift at a later date. Unless the charity has reason to believe that the donor will specify a permanent restriction, the contribution should be reported as an increase in temporarily-restricted net assets pending the donor's purpose restriction. If, at the future date, the donor specifies that the charity can use the net assets for its unrestricted use, the expiration of the donor restriction is reported. Also see the discussion of donor advised funds on pages 20-21 and 69-71.

Penalty clauses in restricted grants. Some donors include penalty clauses in their restricted grants that spell out the consequences if the charities do not abide by the donors' restrictions. Those penalty clauses generally are applicable for long-term contributions or permanent endowments. For example, a donor could require a charity that invades the corpus of a permanent endowment to return the contribution plus interest. Those penalties do not prevent a charity from recognizing contribution revenue at the time the contribution is received. Non-compliance with donor-imposed restrictions may result in a loss contingency requiring either recognition of a liability or disclosure in the financial statements.[68]

Accounting records for restricted gifts. Adequate records should be maintained to document all donor-restricted gifts:

- **Temporarily-restricted gifts.** Records should be retained for each temporarily-restricted project until all project funds have been expended and the annual independent audit has been completed for the time period in which the funds were received and expended. For the auditor to test donor restrictions, it is generally important to retain the donation data and the response forms (the data and response forms will often be retained electronically). It is often appropriate to maintain the records by project for several years to support the use of the gifts within the donor-imposed restrictions.

- **Permanently-restricted gifts.** The recordkeeping requirement for permanently-restricted gifts is generally much greater than for temporarily-restricted gifts. Retaining records related to permanently-restricted gifts is important for audit purposes and also to provide documentation to support the use of the gifts within the donor-imposed restrictions. The file should include information about the initial gift(s) from the donor(s) for the specific purpose; annual documentation on additional gifts to the fund; earnings on fund investments and disbursements.

Earnings on restricted funds. Charities have historically viewed interest and dividend income from permanently-restricted endowment funds as "spendable" capital appreciation remaining a part of the restricted fund. However, the Uniform Management of Institutional Funds Act (UMIFA), which has been adopted by most states, incorporates a "total return" measure that considers realized and unrealized capital gains and losses in measuring return on investment. Thus, charities subject to the UMIFA are permitted to treat capital appreciation on restricted funds as unrestricted or temporarily-restricted income (assuming the donor has not specifically restricted the use of the appreciation or that state law does not impose other restrictions) if the charity's board determines this treatment is prudent.

UMIFA has not been adopted in all states, and the format in some states restricts its application. Before relying on the total return concept, an organization should confirm that UMIFA applies to its endowment fund.

Although UMIFA incorporates the total return concept, the UMIFA and state laws still require that the money be held or spent only in accordance with the restrictions imposed by the donor.

A comprehensive revision of UMIFA, called the Uniform Prudent Management of Institutional Funds Act (UPMIFA), was approved by state law commissioners on July 13, 2006 at the National Conference of Commissioners on Uniform State Laws (NCCUSL) annual meeting. The act will be introduced into the legislature of each jurisdiction. If signed into law, UPMIFA will replace UMIFA, which has been the standard.

UPMIFA would have widespread implications for charities, including:

- Elimination of the historic dollar value limitation on spending (the so-called "underwater funds" rule—see Glossary for "underwater funds" and the "underwater funds rule").

- Broadening the scope covered by the statute, which is intended to apply to trusts, governmental agencies, and any other type of entity dedicated to charitable purposes, as well as nonprofit organizations.
- Comprehensive incorporation of modern portfolio investment standards by providing for diversification of assets, pooling of assets, total return investment and whole portfolio management.
- Endorsing the concept of intergenerational equity via an optional provision that allows states to find that an organization spending more than seven percent of its endowment in one year is acting imprudently.

Accounting issues for deputized fund-raising. Gifts to a charity preferenced to support particular workers such as missionaries, are generally considered to be temporarily restricted under Generally Accepted Accounting Principles (GAAP) because the purpose of the gift is more narrow than the general purposes of the charity while still meeting the IRS requirements for charitable contributions.

Because of the unique circumstances surrounding projects and support of missionaries in the field, a charity should have sufficient discretion and control over gifts to permit the charity to redirect the gifts for other missionaries (for example, redirection of funds often occurs when a missionary separates service with the charity). This redirection does not negate or negatively impact the charitable nature of the gifts. Rather, it is a clear demonstration of a charity properly exercising discretion and control over gifts.

There are certain other accounting issues that should be considered when using the deputized fund-raising concept.

1. **Revenue vs. agency treatment.** The IRS takes the position that in order for the gifts to be tax-deductible contributions (rather than nondeductible gifts to individuals), charities must have adequate control and discretion over the funds to use them exclusively for exempt purposes. Although there are separate tax and accounting rules applicable to gifts raised under the deputized fund-raising concept, if a gift is treated as a nondeductible earmarked transaction (see Chapter 5) for tax purposes, it will

generally be reported as an agency transaction for accounting purposes. Conversely, a gift that qualifies for a charitable deduction under the tax rules is generally a contribution under the accounting rules. Thus, gifts that support the organization's programs, preferenced for specific workers should generally be treated as revenues and expenses of the charity only if they represent contributions to the charity.

Gifts over which a charity has discretion and control should generally not be treated as agency funds (recorded as a liability). Such treatment is a strong indication the funds were earmarked for a specific individual rather than given for the benefit of the charity. Agency treatment of deputized funds raised may jeopardize the tax-deductibility of the gift.

The issuance of charitable receipts should be consistent with the accounting treatment of the gifts:

- Preferenced gifts over which the charity exercises adequate control and discretion should generally be recorded as gift revenue and the donor should be provided a charitable receipt.

- Earmarked gifts should generally be recorded as a liability and charitable receipts should not be issued.

2. **Separate accounts for each worker.** Charities may wish to utilize separate accounts for each deputized worker. This treatment should not jeopardize the donor's charitable tax deduction as long as the ministry maintains control and discretion over the funds.

3. **Pledges vs. intentions to give.** Support raised for deputized workers may be done on a pledge or intention-to-give basis. Pledges made by a donor are unconditional promises to give. Amounts pledged should be recorded as revenue at fair value at the time the pledge is made to the charity.

   In determining the fair value of an unconditional promise or pledge, charities should consider the present value of expected cash flows. In considering measurement of expected cash flows for unconditional promises, charities should consider the likelihood that the donor may discontinue payments at some point due to circumstances such as financial hardship, death of the donor, discontinuance of a program or key individual, or for other reasons. However, communications from donors which express only an intention to give (often termed "faith promises") are not recorded in the accounting records until the gift is collected or until an unconditional promise to give is made.

4. **Unrestricted vs. temporarily restricted treatment.** For a gift raised under the deputized fund-raising concept to qualify for a charitable deduction, the donor cannot restrict the use of the funds for a particular worker. Gifts given to a charity, over which the charity exercises adequate discretion and control, may qualify for a charitable deduction if the donor indicates a preference to support the work of a particular individual but the donor's intent is to benefit the charity.

   A donor's preference generally does not restrict a gift. However, the request for a deputized fund-raising gift generally identifies the activities of a particular work with sufficient specificity to qualify the gift for temporarily restricted treatment. In these instances, the gift is restricted to an activity (the gift may also be limited to a particular location or region-in effect, a double restriction) even though the preferencing does not create a restriction.

   The classification of a gift does not change from temporarily restricted to unrestricted because the charity exercises adequate discretion and control over a donor-preferenced gift (for example, the charity has the right to redirect a preferenced gift to a deputized worker or benevolent recipient other than the individual preferenced by the donor). Neither does the classification of a gift change from temporarily restricted to unrestricted because a charity exercises discretion and control over a gift that has been restricted for a particular activity.

Accounting for short-term mission trips. Gifts that qualify for the issuance of charitable gift receipts by a charity should be recorded as charitable gift revenue by the sponsoring organization. If earmarked gifts are accepted by the sponsoring organization, the amounts should generally be treated as agency funds and reflected as a liability on the organization's statement of financial position.

Some sponsoring organizations, initially record gifts preferenced for particular trip participants as a liability until the trip is complete and then reclassify the transaction as a charitable gift. This is done in an effort to justify any refunds for gifts preferenced for potential trip participants who did not go on the trip. This practice is inconsistent with the need to exercise discretion and control over the gifts, could jeopardize the charitable deductibility of the gifts, and the practice is not recommended.

Gifts for short-term mission trips will generally qualify for recording as temporarily-restricted revenue. This is because a short-term mission trip usually represents a purpose that is more specific than the broad limits imposed by the charity's purpose and nature (see pages 6-8).

Chapter Review 9

1. How are temporarily-restricted gifts reflected on the statement of activities and/or in the footnotes of the financial statements? They should be recognized as temporarily-restricted income when the gifts are received or unconditionally promised.

2. How are temporarily-restricted gifts reflected on the statement of financial position? If the gifts have not been used for the stipulated purpose at the reporting date, the amounts should be displayed on the statement of financial position as part of the temporarily-restricted net assets.

3. Should temporarily-restricted gifts (and related expenses) be separately recorded in the accounting records even if the charity anticipates expending all of the funds in the current accounting period? Yes, it is appropriate to separately record the data regardless of when the use of the funds is anticipated. If the criteria to reflect the data as unrestricted activity are met, this may be done. If the criteria are not met, the appropriate reflection of temporarily-restricted activity may be shown.

4. How are expenses relating to the use of donor-restricted gifts reflected on the statement of activities? They are reflected as unrestricted expenses after reclassifications are made based on expenditures that fulfill donor-imposed purpose restrictions or the expiration of time restrictions.

5. If a gift is treated as an earmarked transaction, not qualifying for a charitable gift deduction under the tax rules, how is the gift recorded for accounting purposes? The gift should generally be reported as an agency transaction. Conversely, a gift that qualifies for a charitable deduction under the accounting rules is generally contribution income under the accounting rules.

6. Does a donor have the power to restrict otherwise unrestricted net assets? Yes. A donor may make a restricted contribution that is conditioned on the charity restricting a certain amount of its unrestricted net assets. If the charity accepts the gift, the restrictions are not reversible without the donor's consent and result in a reclassification of unrestricted net assets to temporarily- or permanently-restricted net assets.

7. Are earnings on restricted gifts also restricted? Generally, no. However, in some situations, the Uniform Management of Institutional Funds Act has implications for permanently-restricted endowment funds.

8. Should gifts received under the deputized fund-raising approach be reflected as revenue or liabilities? Gifts that are subject to the charity's discretion and control generally qualify for recording as revenues. Nondeductible earmarked gifts should generally be recorded as liabilities.

9. Are deputized fund-raising gifts unrestricted or temporarily restricted for accounting purposes? It depends. The preferencing of a gift to support a particular worker generally does not restrict a gift. However, the request for a deputized fund-raising gift generally identifies the activities of a particular work with sufficient specificity to qualify the gift for temporarily-restricted treatment. In these instances, the gift is restricted to an activity (the gift may also be limited to a particular location or region—in effect, a double restriction) even though the preferencing does not create a restriction.

Chapter 10

Special Donor-Restricted Gift Issues

Executive Summary

- Donors of restricted gifts must generally be notified of the fair market value of goods or services given to the donor in exchange for the gifts. Only the excess of any money and the value of any property contributed above the value of goods or services is deductible as a charitable contribution.

- Charities should provide a report to donors, upon request, on the total amount donated for projects to demonstrate a charity's accountability.

- It is appropriate for a charity to pay a tithe on donor-restricted gifts if the charity has communicated that the tithing policy will be applied to restricted gifts.

- Gift catalog solicitations should generally include a disclaimer statement. When a cafeteria of gift options is offered in the catalog, it is difficult to project which ones will be selected by donors. Thus, donors may "purchase" more items than can be practically delivered and used. A properly worded and communicated disclaimer generally gives the charity the necessary flexibility in applying excess gift "purchases" to other items that are needed.

- Charities are legally required to spend restricted net assets to further the intent and purposes expressed by the donor. Therefore, interorganizational loans from restricted net assets should be avoided.

- Gifts to support disaster relief generally qualify as a charitable deduction if the funds are provided to a group of individuals large or indefinite enough that providing aid to members of the class benefits the community as a whole.

A number of special issues are often associated with donor-restricted gifts. For example, a part-restricted gift/part-purchase transaction may raise quid pro quo issues. Or, the borrowing of funds that had been given as donor-restricted gifts and used for operational purposes raises other issues.

Benefits provided to donors of restricted gifts. A taxpayer may not deduct a gift as a restricted (or unrestricted) charitable contribution if the taxpayer receives a substantial benefit (other than intangible benefits or items of token value) for the gift to the charitable organization.[69]

If the size of a taxpayer's gift to a charity is clearly out of proportion to the benefit received, the taxpayer may claim a charitable contribution equal to the difference between the gift to the charitable organization and the fair value of the benefit received on the theory that the funds have the "dual character" of a purchase and a contribution. Such a benefit is often referred to as a "quid pro quo."

Any charitable organization soliciting quid pro quo contributions (restricted or unrestricted) in excess of $75 must provide a written statement that

- Informs the donor that the amount of the gift deductible as a charitable contribution is limited to the amount of any money and the value of any property contributed above the value of goods or services furnished in return (quid pro quo), *and*
- Includes a good-faith estimate of the value of the quid pro quo.

This disclosure may be furnished either in connection with the solicitation or with the receipt of the gift. This statement should be provided shortly after a contribution is received by the charity. Even so, the IRS has indicated generally that it would prefer the disclosure be made at the same time the contribution is solicited.[70]

The statement must be in writing and should be made in a manner that will be recognized by the donor. For example, a disclosure in small print within a larger document might not meet this requirement.

A charity is required to provide this disclosure statement only once, either with the solicitation or shortly after the receipt of a contribution. In addition, if the contribution is $250 or more, the donor must have a receipt from the charity to substantiate this deduction. The disclosure and the donor-receipting rules do not require the same information nor are they required to be sent to the donor at the same time. Thus, it may be more practical to make quid pro quo disclosures with solicitations and tailor receipts sent to donors around the donor-receipting rules.

Reports for donor-restricted projects. ECFA's Standard 7.6 requires a charity to provide a report, on request, on the amount donated for a particular project, the costs related to administering the project, and the amounts going to the project for which the solicitation was made. Project reports should communicate project results to donors as an evidence of a charity's accountability.

While Standard 7.6 only requires project reports be provided on request, proactive charities send donors reports and/or post project updates on their website to communicate project results to donors in a timely manner.

A "project" generally occurs when a donor places a restriction on a gift as to purpose or time, or a charity accepts contributions that are solicited with a time limitation or for an area of program services, such as a specific project. Solicitation for project-related gifts may occur via fund-raising events, through direct mail, through Internet solicitation, by radio or television and in other ways. Such donations are generally considered "temporarily restricted."

Unrestricted contributions have no implicit or explicit time or donor restrictions and are available to be used at any time and in any exempt area or operation of the organization. Therefore, project reporting does not apply to unrestricted gifts.

The report should include the amount of donated income, the costs related to administering the project, and the amounts that went directly to the project for which the solicitation was held. Any unusual items related to income or disbursements should be identified and explained. Financial statements provide overall financial data for the reporting period but are not intended to provide data on specific projects. In addition to financial reports, project accomplishments should be shared with the donor. This may include both short-term and long-range results of project gifts.

The appropriate style of the project report depends on various factors. If the donor's request is in writing, a written response is generally appropriate. If the request is made by telephone, a verbal response may be adequate. Some charities may post project information on their websites to reduce the need to provide written and verbal responses. If the project reporting is made "widely available" or the charity is subject to a "harassment campaign," the Internet reporting generally satisfies reasonable disclosure.

The primary responsibility for project reporting is to a charity's donors. Any information that is shared with individuals who have not donated to a certain project may be appropriate, but it is not required as a commitment to financial accountability.

Paying tithes on restricted gift revenue. Some charities desire to give a tithe of what they receive to another charity. This is often based on their sincere belief that the scriptural principles of tithing extend to their ministry income. Before a charity adopts a tithing policy, it should consider certain issues.

When a donor makes a gift to a charity, the gift must be used by the charity in the furtherance of its tax-exempt purposes—whether or not the gift is restricted. (See pages 5-8 for the impact of a charity's purpose in comparison to a gift.)

If charity A tithes to charity B from unrestricted funds, care must be taken to assure that funds expended by charity B are not for charitable purposes more broad than charity A's charitable purposes.

Non-gift income such as product sales, rental income, and investment income are not tied to donor expectations. Thus, a charity may have more flexibility to use these funds as the source of a tithe as long as charity B expends the funds within charity A's tax-exempt purpose.

Tithing on donor-restricted gifts is only appropriate if the charity has clearly communicated in solicitations that the tithing policy will be applied to restricted gifts. Otherwise, when a donor gives a gift for a specific purpose, it becomes a restriction that those funds be spent for the stated purpose only.

If a charity decides to adopt a tithing policy that includes donor's gifts, it is important that the charity properly communicate this policy to its donors. This should be done at least annually through venues such as annual reports, fund-raising appeals, or gift receipts.

Gift catalogs. Some charities use a gift catalog concept to communicate specific needs to donors. Donors have the opportunity to fund a goat or a cow, buy a month of tutoring for a child, buy a fruit tree, buy a pediatric wheelchair, dig a well, or build a new home for a needy family. Gift catalogs that use these types of projects generate temporarily-restricted gifts.

There are several pertinent issues associated with fund-raising via gift catalogs to assure compliance with ECFA's fund-raising standards:

- **Gifts exceeding the need.** A disclaimer statement should explain what will happen if the total amount received for a particular item exceeds funding needs for that project. Generally, excess gifts should be used to provide similar assistance to people in different locations or used to meet additional needs in that same project. For example, if more wells are purchased than needed in the course of a year, additional funding will meet other needs of the individuals in those particular programs.

- **Gifts insufficient to meet the need.** A disclaimer statement should explain what will occur if the total amount received for a particular item is insufficient to meet the funding needs for the item, *e.g.,* the donor purchases a "share" in building a home for a needy family. Four shares are required to build the home and only two shares are donated. The disclaimer might state that if not enough shares are given to cover the full cost of an item, shares will be pooled with the charity's other funding sources to meet the goals of a similar project.

- **Inclusion in price of gift.** Gift amounts often include the actual and management (overhead) costs associated with purchasing and/or delivering an item or carrying out the service. It reflects the total amount needed to make that specific activity happen, whether it's shipping and distributing pharmaceuticals or building a home for an orphan.

While gift catalogs can be an effective fund-raising tool, the concept often requires significant monitoring to assure that funds are spent in compliance with the donor's restrictions.

Borrowing restricted funds. When a charity's finances are tight, it is possible to deplete unrestricted net assets. At that point, charities may be tempted to borrow cash held for donor-restricted net assets to cover operating expenses. These borrowings are often referred to as an "intraorganizational" loan.[71] Charities are legally required to spend restricted net assets to further the intent and purposes expressed by the donor. Therefore, loans from restricted net assets should be avoided.

Intraorganizational loans are often more troublesome than other types of loans. State laws generally require that a charity demonstrate that a loan (an investment transaction from the standpoint of the restricted fund) is prudent. If the loan is simply to fund operating shortfalls or reflecting the organization's financial difficulties, the charity's board will generally have trouble demonstrating that a loan from restricted net assets is prudent as viewed from the restricted fund's vantage point.

Intraorganizational loans are also tainted with the duality of interests. It is very difficult for a charity's board to be objective when they are simultaneously responsible for the prudent investment of restricted funds and responsible for the proper overall operation of the charity.

Charities often make intraorganizational loans without realizing they have done so. A simple way to determine if a charity is borrowing from restricted net assets is to compare temporarily- and permanently-restricted net assets to total cash plus marketable securities plus any assets specifically termed restricted. If the restricted net asset amount is greater than the sum of the other amounts, is it very likely that borrowing has occurred.

Although loans from restricted net assets should be avoided, if a charity does borrow restricted net assets, financial reports provided to the board should clearly reflect the borrowing. The board should adopt appropriate policies with respect to the borrowing of restricted net assets to ensure the funds are repaid within a reasonable period of time.

Restricted gifts used to fund a charity's budget. When a donor restricts a gift for a segment of a charity's budget, clarity in the communication between the donor and the charity is necessary to ensure honoring the donor's wishes.

Example 1: A donor makes a $1,000 contribution to a church for its youth program. The youth budget for the year is $5,000. If it is the donor's understanding that the $1,000 will merely help fund the youth budget for the year, the gift may be used in that way.

Example 2: A donor makes a $10,000 contribution to a church for its youth program. The youth budget for the year is $25,000. The donor specifies the $10,000 must be used over and above the $25,000 budget. Some churches may reject this gift because it gives the donor power to significantly over-ride the budget. However, if the gift is accepted with the stated condition, the church must spend the $10,000 above the amount budgeted.

Prohibiting the acceptance of restricted gifts. Occasionally a charity will adopt a policy prohibiting restricted gifts to the charity. The prohibition may be stated in a policy by the governing board or other administrative policy. What impact does this type of policy have on a donor's gift? It depends on the understanding between the donor and the donee.

The mere fact the charity has a policy not to honor restricted gifts does not supercede the donor's gift restriction unless the charity's policy is clearly communicated to donors. A "Yes" answer to *all* of the following questions would be helpful to support a charity's policy on prohibiting restricted gifts:

- Do all appeals for fund gifts (from the pulpit, in written solicitations, etc.) clearly and explicitly express the charity's policy that it will not accept any restricted gifts?

- Are offering envelopes and other response vehicles devoid of any option to restrict gifts for missions, buildings, etc.?

- Are charitable gift receipts devoid of any indication of restriction limitations?

- If the charity receives a gift with a donor restriction, do they refund the money or offer to refund it unless the donor agrees to remove the gift restriction?

It is difficult to adequately communicate a "no restricted gifts" policy to all donors. Additionally, the charity's communication is simply part of the equation; a donor's intent relates both to what is communicated in an appeal and to any donor instructions accompanying the gift. On balance, charities are better served to proactively approve projects to which donors can restrict their gifts.

Some charities include provisions in their governing documents or board resolutions indicating the organization retains the right to modify conditions on the use of assets (sometimes called "variance powers"). Such powers should be clearly communicated to donors.

Disaster relief. Gifts for disaster relief often meet the donor-restricted gift definition, *e.g.*, gifts are restricted for purposes more specific than the broad limits imposed by the charity's purpose and nature.

The IRS provides excellent guidance on the disaster relief topic,[72] especially in the areas of:

- **Charitable class.** The group of individuals that may properly receive assistance from a charity is called a charitable class. A charitable class must be *large* or *indefinite* enough that providing aid to members of the class benefits the community as a whole. Because of this requirement, a charity involved in disaster relief or emergency hardship cannot target and limit its assistance to specific individuals, such as a few persons injured in a particular fire.

  Similarly donors cannot earmark contributions to a charity for a particular individual or family. When a disaster or emergency hardship occurs, a charity may help individuals who are needy or otherwise distressed because they are part of a general class of charitable beneficiaries, provided the charity selects who gets the assistance.

- **Needy or distressed test.** Generally, a charity involved in disaster relief or emergency hardship must make a specific assessment that a recipient of aid is financially or otherwise in need. Individuals do not have to be totally destitute to be financially needy; they may merely lack the resources to obtain basic necessities.

  Charitable funds cannot be distributed to individuals merely because they are victims of a disaster. Therefore, an organization's decision about how its funds will be distributed must be based on an objective evaluation of the victim's needs at the time the grant is made. The scope of the assessment required to support the need for assistance may vary depending upon the circumstances.

A charity may provide crisis counseling, rescue services, or emergency aid such as blankets or hot meals without a showing of financial need. The individuals requiring these services are distressed irrespective of financial condition. In contrast, providing three to six months of financial assistance to families to pay for basic housing because of a disaster or emergency hardship would require a financial need assessment before disbursing aid.

- **Short- and long-term assistance.** Often charities are established (or programs are established by charities) as a result of a particular disaster where both short-term and long-term assistance might be required. The following types of assistance, if based on individual need, would be consistent with charitable purposes:

  ✓ assistance to allow a surviving spouse with young children to remain at home with the children to maintain the psychological well-being of the entire family

  ✓ assistance with elementary and secondary school tuition and higher education costs to permit a child to attend a school

  ✓ assistance with rent, mortgage payments, or car loans to prevent loss of a primary home or transportation that would cause additional trauma to families already suffering

  ✓ travel costs for family members to attend funerals and to provide comfort to survivors

- **Documentation of disaster relief payments.** A charity must maintain adequate records that demonstrate the victims' needs for the assistance provided. These records must also show that the charity's payments further charitable purposes. Thus, records are required when aid is provided to individuals based on a specific assessment of need.

  Documentation should include:

  ✓ a complete description of the assistance

- ✓ the purpose for which the aid was given
- ✓ the charity's objective criteria for disbursing assistance under each program
- ✓ how the recipients were selected
- ✓ the name, address, and the amount distributed to each recipient
- ✓ any relationship between a recipient and officers, directors, or key employees of or substantial contributions to the charity

A charity that is distributing short-term emergency assistance would only be expected to maintain records such as the type of assistance provided, criteria for disbursing assistance, date, place, estimated number of victims assisted (individual names and addresses are not required), charitable purpose intended to be accomplished, and the cost of the aid. Examples, of such short-term emergency aid would include blankets, hot meals, electric fans, or coats, hats, and gloves. A charity that is distributing longer-term aid should keep the above more-detailed records.

Chapter Review 10

1. Are charities required to notify the donor that the amount of the gift that is deductible as a charitable contribution is limited to the amount of any money and the value of any property contributed above the value of goods or services furnished in return? Yes. Additionally, the charity must provide a good-faith estimate of the value (not the cost) of the goods or services furnished to the donor.

2. Must charities provide a report to donors who make gifts to a project? ECFA members are required to do so, upon written request, and it is a best practice for all charities.

3. May charities pay a tithe on donor-restricted revenue? Not unless the charity has clearly communicated the tithing policy will be applied to restricted gifts.

4. May a charity borrow from donor-restricted resources to pay operating expenses? Charities are legally required to spend restricted net assets to further the intent and purposes expressed by the donor. Therefore, loans from restricted net assets should be avoided.

5. A donor restricts a gift for the church's youth program. Is it appropriate for the church to simply use the gift as part of the funding for the youth program budget, which would otherwise primarily be funded from unrestricted gifts? It depends. If the donor restricted the gift for purposes over and above the amount the church budgeted for the youth program (or understood the gift would be used in that manner), then the gift must be used to fund expenses *not* included in the budget. If the donor understood the gift would simply be used to fund the amount budgeted for the youth program, the funds could be used in that manner.

Exhibits

Sample Gift Acceptance Guidelines

A charity should evaluate the following factors in considering potential gifts:

- Whether the gift is consistent with the charity's tax-exempt purposes
- Whether the charity can exercise sufficient control over the gift
- Whether the gift does not have the characteristics of an earmarked transaction
- Whether it will cost the charity money to own the asset
- Whether it will cost the charity money to sell the asset
- Staff and volunteer time required to manage or sell the asset
- Whether owning or selling the asset will expose the charity to liability
- The marketability of the asset and the cash flow it can be expected to generate

A gift acceptance policy will typically list various asset types and describe how the charity will handle proposed gifts of each type, based on the factors above. The following are just a few examples of gift types:

- **Real estate.** There are often costs associated with owning and selling real estate. Cost of owning real estate includes insurance, maintenance and property taxes. Cost of selling may include sales commissions, title fees, and inspections.

  The risks associated with environmental issues may be significant. Even if the charity is in the chain of title, it could be exposed to liability of toxins on the property under state and federal environmental laws.

  Marketability may be a challenge for a charity, especially with commercial property or undeveloped land. Selling residential property in a down market may also be an issue.

A charity should check for any mortgages or liens on the property which will be paid out of sale proceeds. It should also review any leases or contracts to which the property is subject.

- **Closely held businesses.** Donated stock in corporations that are not listed on stock exchanges, partnerships and limited liability corporations require special evaluation. Marketability can be a challenge since the potential buyers are generally the other owners of the business who may be relatives of the donor. Small business owners often enter into agreements with the other owners which limit their ability to sell.

  Many small businesses, including partnerships, limited liability corporation and "S" corporations (corporations described in subchapter S of the Internal Revenue Code) pass taxable income through to the owners. For a charity, income from a pass-through entity may be subject to unrelated business income tax.

- **Life insurance.** It is generally acceptable for a donor to name a charity as a beneficiary of his or her life insurance; this puts no obligation on the charity. But if the charity is given a policy or asked to enter into any kind of contract, the charity should review the documents carefully and make sure it understands how the arrangement will work and what the costs and risks are.

Sample Overhead Communication to Donors

What is our overhead rate? We take seriously our responsibility to be good stewards of the funds entrusted to us. We are accountable to our donors, the recipients of our ministry and God to use them wisely. We continually strive to keep our overhead low without sacrificing the structures and staff needed to maintain a high level of ministry. Last year, we used nearly 80 percent of our total revenue (which included the use of both cash donations and the value of donated food, clothing, medicine, and other goods) to benefit ministry recipients.

Overhead and effectiveness. Overhead is only one consideration in choosing a charity to support. Much more important is the charity's mission and how effectively it accomplishes that mission. Results, impact, efficient management, and fiscal controls all are factors in an organization's effectiveness. Despite the implied message by Internet rating groups, the most effective charity is not necessarily the one with the lowest overhead rate. A reasonable amount of overhead is needed to achieve ministry objectives.

While we openly share our overhead rate of 20 percent, we recognize that overhead rates alone are inadequate for evaluating a charity. Accounting practices and the method of delivering programs vary from organization to organization, making an across-the-board comparison based on overhead impossible.

The impact of resources on overhead. A charity's overhead rate is often influenced by its primary sources of donations. The cost of procuring gifts-in-kind, such as high-value medicines and equipment, is very low. Securing government grants also requires a smaller investment than does raising donations through direct mail.

Since the use of gifts-in-kind are generally categorized as program expense, a charity with significant gifts-in-kind revenue (and expense) will almost always have a lower overhead rate compared with a similar type organization that does not receive significant gifts-in-kind.

Note: As a matter of transparency, it is often wise the share information about an organization's overhead rate with donors. Informed donors know overhead is required to effectively operate a charity. By communicating the organization's overhead rate and its implications on the charity, many donors will have a greater respect for the charity.

Sample Wording for Deputized Fund-Raising Letters

The following are examples of wording that may demonstrate the charity's discretion and control (or the lack of the same) over funds raised under the deputized concept:

Appropriate Wording	Inappropriate Wording
• Please continue to pray that the last 50% of the support I am responsible to raise for ABC Mission comes in soon.	• Please continue to pray the last 50% of my support comes in soon.
• Seventy-five percent of the support I need to raise for ABC Mission has been committed.	• I am at 75% of my needed funds raised.
• It is my responsibility to form a team of ministry partners who will support ABC Mission with monthly gifts and prayers.	• I need a team of ministry partners who will support me with monthly pledges and prayers.
• Please make your gift to ABC Mission preferenced for my support	• Please designate your gift for my support.

Sample Deputized Fund-Raising Letter

Version A

This letter demonstrates elements consistent with IRS guidance.

We are thrilled to send you our first letter since arriving here in Sumy, Ukraine. The flight was long but uneventful, and we are getting settled into the house provided by Missions International.

It is not possible for Nancy and me to adequately express our appreciation for your willingness to provide prayer and financial support for the ministry here. Your liberal gifts to support the outreach ministry of Missions International in Sumy enables us to serve here.

> The wording makes it clear that Bill and Nancy are serving under the auspices of the missionary organization.

The Missions International field in Sumy includes a church, school and a ministry center. All three units of the ministry are in the early stages of development so we have our work cut out for us to help bring maturity to these programs.

Missions International is a faith mission organization. As staff members, we must develop financial partnerships to provide the funding for salary, ministry expenses, health benefits, and related expenses. A portion of each gift dollar goes to administrative costs.

> The employer-employee relationship is documented here. This paragraph even goes beyond the guidance outlined by the IRS and discloses that a portion of the gift will be used for overhead.

In service to the Master,

Bill and Nancy Jones

Sample Deputized Fund-Raising Response Form

Version A

We believe in the work of Missions International and are sending our gift of $____________.

We would like our gift to benefit the ministry of Bill and Nancy Jones in Sumy, Ukraine. We understand that the use of the gift is subject to the discretion and control of Missions International.

> These paragraphs make it clear that the donor's intent is to benefit the charity. Their financial support of Bill and Nancy Jones is simply a desire.

Donor(s):
Jim and Ren Gilfouile
285 Shortridge Road
Indianapolis, IN 46218

Sample Deputized Fund-Raising Gift Acknowledgment

Version A

Official Receipt • Please keep this receipt for your tax records

Receipt #7639 Date: 01/31/08 Jim and René Gilfouile 285 Shortridge Road Indianapolis, IN 46218	Gift Purpose Preferenced for the work carried out by: Bill and Nancy Jones	Total Amount	Gift Amount	Other Amount
		$100	**$100**	**0**

Thank you for your contribution which is tax-deductible to the extent allowed by law. While every effort will be made to apply your gift according to an indicated preference, if any, **Missions International** has complete discretion and control over the use of the donated funds. We recognize our responsibility for accountability and our audited financial statements are available upon request. We thank God for you and appreciate your support.

Missions International
PO Box 5646
Yakima, WA 98904
509/248-0000

Other than reflected on this receipt, no goods or services, in part or in whole, were provided in exchange for this gift.

Sample Deputized Fund-Raising Letter

Version B

This letter is not compliant with IRS guidance.

Hi! Meet our family. John is 18 and a freshman in college, Joshua is 16 and a high school junior, Andy is 12 and in 7th grade, and Macy turns 4 on July 2!

For the past eight years, we have served as missionaries to India. We are more convinced than ever that this is where God wants us to be at this time. We are helping existing churches plant 7,000 new churches.

We are working on a plan to select, train, and empower more leaders in India. This will be a long process of developing leaders to the point where they can be entrusted with major responsibilities, so pray that God will provide the right people, for the right roles, at the right time.

We would love to have you partner with us as we continue to follow Jesus. If you can support us in the battle for souls in India by providing for our financial needs with your generous gifts, we will certainly appreciate it. It is a joy to serve Christ with you as partners in ministry.

Henry and Mary Miller

The letter does not mention the name of the charity under which they are serving or state that gifts to the charity are needed so their work may continue. Direct support is requested for Henry and Mary Miller instead of support for the employing charity. The response form clarifies these issues, but the communication of this issue could be strengthened by including references in both the letter and the response form.

Sample Deputized Fund-Raising Response Form

Version B

We want to support the ministry of a Missions Worldwide missionary with our gift of $______________. We would like for our gift to benefit the ministry of Henry and Mary Miller and the work in India.

We understand that the use of our gift is subject to the discretion and control of Missions Worldwide.

Donor(s):
Ed and Sherry Workman
2523 East 9th Avenue
Wauchula, FL 32578

> These paragraphs make it clear that the donor's intent is to benefit the charity. Their financial support of Henry and Mary Miller is simply a desire.

Sample Deputized Fund-Raising Gift Acknowledgment

Version B

Official Receipt • Please keep this receipt for your tax records

Receipt #7639 Date: 01/31/08 Ed and Sherry Workman 2523 East 9th Avenue Wauchula, FL 32578	Gift Purpose Preferenced for the work carried out by: Henry and Mary Miller	Total Amount **$100**	Gift Amount **$100**	Other Amount **0**

Thank you for your contribution which is tax-deductible to the extent allowed by law. While every effort will be made to apply your gift according to an indicated preference, if any, **Missions Worldwide** has complete discretion and control over the use of the donated funds. We recognize our responsibility for accountability and our audited financial statements are available upon request. We thank God for you and appreciate your support.

Other than reflected on this receipt, no goods or services, in part or in whole, were provided in exchange for this gift.

Missions Worldwide
PO Box 5646
Yakima, WA 98904
509/248-0000

Sample Deputized Fund-Raising Letter

Version C

This letter demonstrates elements that are inconsistent with IRS guidance.

We are thrilled to send you our first letter since arriving here in Mexico City, Mexico as independent missionaries.

The word "independent" implies they are not working under the auspices of a missionary organization.

The wording connotes a personal ministry: "we are opening," "the church God has led us to build," and "contributions for our project."

We are opening an Internet cafe as an outreach ministry. The caf will open doors for the church God has led us to build. To help plant a church here, we ask that you pray about making contributions for our project.

If you want send a gift to us and receive a tax deductible receipt, please send the gift to Conduit International. They only take a three percent administrative fee to cover the processing of gifts and pass through the remainder of the funds to us.

Sending "a gift to us" implies a personal gift that is not tax-deductible. A low administrative fee suggests minimal, if any, oversight. The use of the term "pass through" implies an earmarked transaction.

Gifts to replenish personal savings suggest personal gifts that do not qualify for a charitable deduction.

The needs are so evident and the people so poor that we have used up our saving to help the spread the news of a new church being planted. We could share with you story after story of the needs. To continue this outreach ministry to the needy and local pastors we need your help to replenish our savings account and help with building up a benevolence fund.

This is a mixture of ministry and personal purposes combined under the banner of charitable giving. Requesting funds for a personally-owned is problematic.

We would like to invite new believers to meet in our home so we are looking for a home in the area we could buy and turn into a meeting place. Your contributions to us will help us purchase and remodel a house for this purpose. When we sell the home at the end of our ministry here, the proceeds will provide a reserve which can be used for our retirement.

Thanks so much for your support of our ministry in Mexico City!

In Christian love,

Fred and Rachel Brown

Sample Deputized Fund-Raising Response Form

Version C

We believe in the work you are doing in Mexico City. Here is our gift to you of $______________.

Donor(s):

Greg and Diana Jost
4825 University Street
Newberg, Oregon 97310

Using the reference "to you," the response form indicates a personal nondeductible gift.

Sample Deputized Worker Policy

ABC missionaries are allowed to raise support using various methods and styles. Our support is a provision from God, not from specific donors. Thus, the financial need should be submitted to God through prayer.

Support accounts. When you are approved to raise funds for ABC Mission, an account number will be designated by the Finance Department. Gifts to ABC Mission preferenced to provide the funding necessary to provide compensation, fringe benefits and other expenses in relation to your work with ABC Mission will be credited to this account and expenses relative your employment will be charged to this account.

The balance in the account does not represent your funds. Any donations credited to this account must be donations to support the ministry of ABC Mission, not to you.

If the total amount of the donations recorded in an account is less than the amount budgeted for monthly compensation, only the amount available will be paid. If the total donations recorded are more than the amount budgeted for monthly compensation, the surplus may be used to make up prior shortages and expended for your compensation, fringe benefits and other expenses in relation to your work with ABC Mission. Any surplus may be used in future months for compensation or the surplus may be used by the ministry for other purposes consistent with donor preferences.

Communication to donors. It is essential that you maintain appropriate communication with donors who partner with ABC Mission to provide gifts preferenced for your compensation, fringe benefits and related expenses.

For contributions to be tax-deductible by donors, the gifts must be to ABC Mission and not to or for specific individuals. It is important for donors to understand that ABC Mission has full discretion and control over all contributions. The following guidelines should be followed with respect to terminology used

Sample Deputized Worker Policy *(continued)*

in your prayer letters, email, verbal and other communications with prospective donors to ABC Mission.

A. **Use** the following:

- Pray that God will provide the support I need to raise for ABC Mission.
- Thank you for your prayers and financial gifts to ABC Mission.
- I need to form a team of ministry partners who will support ABC Mission with monthly financial commitments and prayers.
- God has provided 80% of the support I need to raise for ABC Mission.

B. **Avoid** the following:

- Please provide funds for my support.
- I need $1,000 more in gifts to my account.
- My financial support is short this month.
- Please support me.
- My account is short this month.
- Your support of us is appreciated.
- Thanks for your support of my ministry.

Prayer letters. Each staff member who has a support team is allowed one full working day per month to work on raising and maintaining support. This includes writing personal notes to supporters, composing prayer letters, etc. Please keep track of the hours spent on this and report this data annually to the home office. This data will be the basis for allocating a portion of your time to fund-raising expenses on our financial statements.

Prayer letters should periodically be proof read by your department coordinator before the letters are distributed. Prayer letters must be sent every month.

Funds remaining on the date of separation from service. If you terminate with a balance left in the account designated to track contributions and expenses related to the work, ABC

Sample Deputized Worker Policy *(continued)*

Mission reserves the right to use the balance as it deems best. Similarly, if a potential worker is unable to raise the support needed to begin service with ABC Mission and terminates prior to beginning work, ABC Mission may use the funds in the related account as it deems best. The worker is not entitled to receive these funds nor are the donors entitled to refunds.

I have read and understand the above policy and I agree with this policy.

____________ ______________________________

Date **Signature**

Note: See page 88-89 for discussion of policies and communicating them to workers.

Sample Deputized Fund-Raising Gift Check

Bob and Teri Davis
2300 Mission
Wenatchee, WA 98801

Date: *December 31, 2008*

Pay To The Order Of: *ABC Charity* $ *200.00*

Two Hundred and no/100 ---------------------------------- Dollars

For *Missions Work* *Bob Davis*

Note: If a donor wishes to identify the preferenced worker on the check, the "preferential" or "to support the work of" terminology should be used to avoid communicating the gift is earmarked for a particular worker. However, it is generally advisable for the donor to check an appropriately-worded box on the response form indicating a preference to support the ministry of a particular individual.

Sample Deputized Fund-Raising Communication to Donor

ABC Charity

PO Box 5646
Yakima, WA 98904
509/248-0000

Date

Dear Jack and Teri,

Thank you for your recent gift to ABC Charity. Your support is vital for the effective proclamation of the Gospel throughout the world.

On your check or response form, you indicated a preference to support the staff ministry of a particular ABC Charity worker. While we work hard to respect the preferences of each donor and ensure the deductibility of contributions, all gifts must be under the control of the ABC Charity and are not controlled by individual workers. While the use of gifts for ministry conducted by ABC staff are typically used in accordance with donor preferences, at times the board may redirect the use of these gifts.

You are a strategic part of our team, for which we give thanks to Almighty God. May He richly bless your life as you fulfill your gift of giving to Him through the ministry of ABC Charity.

Sincerely,

ABC Charity

Sample Communication to Deputized Workers

ABC Charity
PO Box 5646
Yakima, WA 98904
509/248-0000

Date

Dear Staff,

As a nonprofit organization, ABC Charity is obligated to adhere to specific rules and practices in how we handle the funds donated to ABC Charity to support staff ministry. All gifts must be under control of the organization and not any one individual. We work hard to abide by these expectations while respecting the preferences of each donor.

The IRS often applies two general tests to determine whether a tax-deductible contribution was made to and for the use of a charitable organization or if a gift is a non-deductible pass-through to a particular individual who ultimately benefited from the contribution.

1. The first test is whether the contributor s intent in making the donation was to benefit the organization itself or the individual. The IRS encourages language to the donor such as the following to meet the intended benefit test: This contribution is made with the understanding that the donee organization has complete control and administration over the use of the donated funds.

Page Two

2. The second test is whether the organization has full control of the donated funds and discretion as to their use.

Use appropriate terminology when communicating with donors. Since the organization cannot commit to contributions being paid as salary or expenses to a particular person, deputized workers should never imply the opposite, verbally or in writing. A donor may indicate a preference that a gift to a charity be used to support the ministry of a certain individual and the charity may track the dollars based on the preference.

ABC Charity facilitates donations consistent with ABC compensation and reimbursement guidelines and honors donor preferences to the extent possible. However, all of us need to recognize that these donations should be seen as funds that are legally under the discretion and control of ABC Charity.

Thanks for keeping that in mind as you communicate with your support team.

Your partner in ministry,

ABC Charity

Sample Short-Term Mission Trip Fund-Raising Letter

This short-term mission trip fund-raising letter demonstrates elements which follow IRS guidance. The notes in the letter relate to accounting for the gift and qualifying it for a tax deduction.

1232 Main Street
Yakima, WA 98904
509/248-6739

Date

Dear Mr. and Mrs. Donor,

> This paragraph confirms it is a church-sponsored mission trip.

This summer, I have an exciting opportunity to serve the Lord on a mission trip sponsored by our church (Yakima Fellowship) to East Africa. Fifteen members of my church youth group plan to participate in a 10-day trip. We will fly into Nairobi, Kenya on July 21.

> This paragraph confirms that ministry will be performed on the trip.

Our ministry during this trip is in Nairobi at an orphanage where most of the children have AIDS. Our team will lead a Vacation Bible School, distribute clothes we will take with us, and be available to work with and support the children in the orphanage. Sponsors from our church will accompany our team and provide ministry oversight.

One of the ways you can help me is to pray for the trip, the ministry we will perform and for me personally. Only with a prayer support will I be able to bless the children in the orphanage.

Yes, there are financial needs. The cost of the trip is $2,100, which each team member is responsible to raise in gifts for our church. Please pray with me that the funds to cover my trip expenses will be provided.

This paragraph confirms that gifts are preferenced for Jodi's trip expenses. (For accounting purposes, gifts are temporarily-restricted for the mission trip.)

Gifts to the church, with an expression of a preference for my trip expenses, are tax deductible to the extent allowed by law.

If you will commit to pray, please check the appropriate box on the enclosed card.

This paragraph confirms the church will exercise discretion and control over the funds, implied is: "There are no refunds to donors if I don't go."

If you are able to make a gift to the church to assist with my expenses, please check the appropriate box on the card, indicating your interest in helping fund my portion of the trip expenses, and make your check payable to the sponsoring church, Yakima Fellowship. If I am unable to participate in the trip, your gifts will be used to support the short-term mission program of the church.

May God bless you richly as you consider your involvement in this mission trip!

Sincerely,

Jodi Hunter

Sample Short-Term Mission Trip Response Form (Trip Expenses Paid by the Charity)

We want to support the missions outreach of Yakima Fellowship and are sending our gift of $_____________.

Our preference is that this gift be used to support the short-term mission trip of Jodi Hunter. We understand that the use of the gift is subject to the discretion and control of Yakima Fellowship.

Donor(s):
Bill and Karen Smith
2315 Main
Wenatchee, WA 98801

> These paragraphs make it clear that the donor's intent is to benefit the charity. Their financial support of Jodi Hunter is simply a desire.

Sample Short-Term Mission Trip Gift Acknowledgment (Trip Expenses Paid by the Charity)

Official Receipt • Please keep this receipt for your tax records

Receipt #2675 Date: 01/02/08 Bill and Karen Smith 2315 Main Wenatchee, WA 98801	Preferenced for the mission trip of: Jodi Hunter	Total Amount **$100**	Gift Amount **$100**	Other Amount **0**

Thank you for your contribution which is tax-deductible to the extent allowed by law. While every effort will be made to apply your gift according to an indicated preference, if any, **Yakima Fellowship** has complete discretion and control over the use of the donated funds. We thank God for you and appreciate your support.

No goods or services, in part or in whole, were provided in exchange for this gift.

Yakima Fellowship
PO Box 4256
Yakima, WA 98904
509/248-5555

Sample Short-Term Mission Trip Gift Check (Trip Expenses Paid by the Charity)

Bill and Karen Smith
2315 Main
Wenatchee, WA 98801

DATE: *December 31, 2008*

PAY TO THE ORDER OF: *Yakima Fellowship* $ *200.00*

Two Hundred and no/100 ------------------------------------ DOLLARS

FOR *Missions Work*

Bill Smith

Note: If a donor wishes to identify the preferenced participant on the check, the "preferential" or "to support the trip of" terminology should be used to avoid communicating the gift is earmarked for a particular participant. It is generally more advisable for the donor to check an appropriately-worded box on the response form indicating a preference to support the ministry of a particular trip participant.

Sample Short-Term Mission Trip Gift Acknowledgment (Trip Expenses Paid by the Participant)

Official Receipt • Please keep this receipt for your tax records

Receipt #4575 Date: 08/15/08 Bill and Karen Smith 2315 Main Wenatchee, WA 98801	Description of Services Provided	Built church building in Nairobi, Kenya, on July 21-28, 2008

Thank you for your contribution which are tax-deductible to the extent allowed by law. While every effort will be made to apply your gift according to an indicated preference, if any, **Yakima Fellowship** has complete discretion and control over the use of the donated funds. We thank God for you and appreciate your support.

No goods or services, in part or in whole, were provided in exchange for this gift.

Yakima Fellowship
PO Box 4256
Yakima, WA 98904
509/248-5555

Sample Gift Refund Letter

(Gift refunded in the same year as the donation)

ABC Charity
PO Box 5646
Yakima, WA 98904
509/248-0000

Date

Dear Mr. and Mrs. Donor,

Thank you for your generous gift of $xxx.xx for the XYZ project.

Because (describe the reason for the refund), we are refunding the gift. The amount of the refund will be offset against the gift on your year-end giving statement. Please consider the receipt issued earlier to you for this gift as invalid. The gift does not qualify as a charitable gift for tax deduction purposes.

If you have any questions, please let us know.

Your partner in ministry,

ABC Charity

Note: See pages 46-48, 114 for discussion of refunding gifts.

Sample Gift Refund Letter

(Gift refunded in a year subsequent to the year of the donation)

ABC Charity
PO Box 5646
Yakima, WA 98904
509/248-0000

Date

Dear Mr. and Mrs. Donor,

Thank you for your generous gift of $xxx.xx for the XYZ project. Your gift is being refunded because we were unable to use it for the intended purpose.

Since this refund is issued in a year subsequent to the year of the contribution, you may be obligated to file an amended tax return if you have already deducted the gift on your tax return (alternately, it may be appropriate to include the refunded amount as additional income on Form 1040). The gift does not qualify as a charitable gift for tax deduction purposes in the year in which you made the gift.

Please consider the receipt issued at the time of the gift as invalid. Also, please adjust our year-end giving statement for the year of the gift by the amount of this refund.

If you have any questions, please let us know.

Your partner in ministry,

ABC Charity

Note: See pages 46-48, 114 for discussion of refunding gifts.

Sample Statement of Financial Position

Reporting Restricted Net Assets

	September 30,	
	2008	2007
ASSETS		
Current Assets:		
Cash and cash equivalents	$ 174,300	$ 79,500
Contributions receivable	75,000	74,000
Accounts receivable	234,000	32,500
Prepaid expenses	59,300	63,400
Other	7,500	-
	550,100	249,400
Assets Held in Trust (Note 3)	40,000	-
Property and Equipment—net (Note 4)	1,354,700	1,207,600
Total Assets	$ 1,944,800	$ 1,457,000
LIABILITIES AND NET ASSETS		
Current Liabilities:		
Accounts payable	$ 127,300	$ 76,100
Deferred revenue (Note 2)	150,000	-
Current portion of notes payable (Note 5)	1,500	200
	278,800	76,300
Notes Payable (Note 5)	71,200	3,100
Revocable Trusts (Note 3)	40,000	-
Total Liabilities	390,000	79,400
Net Assets:		
Unrestricted:		
Undesignated	189,800	111,300
Board designated	50,000	50,000
Equity in property and equipment	1,282,000	1,204,300
	1,521,800	1,365,600
Temporarily restricted:		
Expendable (Note 6)	33,000	12,000
Total net assets	1,554,800	1,377,600
Total Liabilities and Net Assets	$ 1,944,800	$ 1,457,000

See notes to financial statements

The financial statements and footnotes on pages 158-59 have been excerpted by permission from the Accounting and Reporting Guide for Christian Ministries.[73]

Sample Statement of Activities

Reporting Restricted Gifts

	Years Ended September 30,					
	2008			2007		
	Unrestricted	Temporarily Restricted	Total	Unrestricted	Temporarily Restricted	Total
Support and Revenue:						
Support:						
Contributions	$ 232,500	$ 279,500	$ 512,000	$ 602,400	$ 16,100	$ 618,500
Donated goods	5,700	-	5,700	101,600	-	101,600
Other grants	26,600	-	26,600	56,300	-	56,300
Special events	1,300	-	1,300	8,800	-	8,800
Contributed skilled services	8,900	-	8,900	8,200	-	8,200
	275,000	279,500	554,500	777,300	16,100	793,400
Revenue:						
Program revenue	230,700		230,700	-		-
Rentals	27,200		27,200	23,900		23,900
Interest	1,500		1,500	3,600		3,600
Other	3,300	-	3,300	-	-	-
	262,700	-	262,700	27,500	-	27,500
Net Assets Released from Restrictions:						
Satisfaction of program restrictions	6,800	(6,800)	-	2,650	(2,650)	-
Satisfaction of development project restrictions	216,000	(216,000)	-	-	-	-
Expiration of time restrictions	8,400	(8,400)	-	-	-	-
Assessments against restricted gifts	27,300	(27,300)	-	1,450	(1,450)	-
Total Support and Revenue	796,200	21,000	817,200	808,900	12,000	820,900

See notes to financial statements

Sample Statement of Activities *(continued)*

	Years Ended September 30,					
	2008			2007		
	Unrestricted	Temporarily Restricted	Total	Unrestricted	Temporarily Restricted	Total
Expenses:						
Program services						
Program A	425,000		425,000	363,500		363,500
Program B	110,000		110,000	21,900		21,900
Program C	36,100	-	36,100	30,700	-	30,700
	571,100	-	571,100	416,100	-	416,100
Supporting activities:						
General and administrative	15,200		15,200	12,800		12,800
Fund-raising	31,600	-	31,600	44,500	-	44,500
	46,800	-	46,800	57,300	-	57,300
Total Expenses	617,900	-	617,900	473,400	-	473,400
Excess of Support and Revenue over Expenses before Extraordinary Loss	178,300	21,000	199,300	335,500	12,000	347,500
Extraordinary Loss on Property (Note 4)	(22,100)	-	(22,100)	-	-	-
Change in Net Assets	156,200	21,000	177,200	335,500	12,000	347,500
Net Assets:						
Beginning of year	1,365,600	12,000	1,377,600	1,030,100	-	1,030,100
End of year	$1,521,800	$33,000	$1,554,800	$1,365,600	$12,000	$1,377,600

Sample Notes to Financial Statements

Reflecting Restricted Net Asset Information

December 31, 2008

Classes of Net Assets

The financial statements report amounts separately by class of net assets.

a) Unrestricted amounts are those currently available at the discretion of the board for use in the organization's operations and those resources invested in equipment.

b) Temporarily-restricted amounts are those that are stipulated by donors for specific operating purposes, the acquisition of equipment, or for use in future accounting periods.

All contributions are considered available for unrestricted use, unless explicitly or implicitly restricted by the donor or subject to other legal restrictions.

Public Support, Revenue, and Expenses

Contributions are reported as income when made, which may be when cash is received, unconditional promises are made, or ownership of donated assets is transferred.

Bequests are recorded as income at the time a right has been established to the bequest and the proceeds are measurable. Noncash gifts are recorded at their estimated fair market value at the date of donation. Contributions restricted by the donor for a specific purpose or for a future accounting period are recorded as revenue in the temporarily-restricted class of net assets until funds have been expended for the purposes specified or the time restrictions have been met. Sales, conference and seminar revenue, and other income are recognized when earned.

Notes to Financial Statements *(continued)*

Membership fees and subscriptions are amortized over the life of the arrangement.

Temporarily-Restricted Net Assets:

Temporarily-restricted net assets represent the unspent balance of donor-restricted contributions for the charity's headquarters development project which was substantially completed during fiscal 2008 and other broadcasting projects. Activity is as follows:

	September 30, 2008	September 30, 2007
Beginning balance	$ 12,000	$ -
Contributions	279,500	16,100
Expenditures (Net assets released from restrictions)	(231,200)	(2,650)
Assessments against restricted gifts	(27,300)	(1,450)
	$ 33,000	$ 12,000

Temporarily-restricted net assets are available for the following purposes or periods:

	September 30, 2008	September 30, 2007
For new Spanish ministry	$ 4,500	$ 2,000
For headquarters development	-	10,000
Equipment stipulated by donor to be used for a minimum of five years	7,500	-
For English ministry to immigrants	21,000	-
	$ 33,000	$ 12,000

Endnotes

[1] L.B. Research and Education Foundation v. UCLA Foundation, 130 Cal. App. 4th 171 (June 14, 2005), in which the court held that a gift created a conditional contract that provided the donor standing to enforce the terms of the gift.

[2] Robertson v. Princeton University (filed July 17, 2002 in Sup. Ct. of N.J.), in which descendants of the donors alleged that Princeton University had commingled funds and failed to fulfill the fund's mission.

In 1961, Charles and Marie Robertson gave Princeton University $35 million in A&P stock—then the largest gift in Princeton's history—to help the U.S. "defend and extend freedom throughout the world by improving the facilities for training and education of men and women for government service."

[3] Financial Accounting Standards Board Statement No. 116, Accounting for Contributions Received and Contributions Made, ¶14

[4] Concept Statement No. 6, par. 95-97, Financial Accounting Standards Board, 1985.

Also, AICPA *Not-for-Profit Audit Guide,* par. 5:38-39, May 2007.

[5] *A General Counsel's Guide to Assessing Restricted Gifts,* "Exempt Organization Tax Review," Michael W. Peregrine and James R. Schwartz, July 2000.

[6] Bank of America National Trust and Savings Association, 326 F.2d 51 at 55, 13 AFTR2d 307 at 311 (CA-9, 1963)

[7] Private Letter Ruling 200250029. In this ruling, donors made a payment to a recognized charity and expressed an interest in supporting the work of a particular composer. The contributions by the donors to the charity were not impermissibly earmarked for the composer, and therefore are a charitable contribution.

[8] Bruce R. Hopkins, *The Law of Tax-Exempt Organizations,* Eighth Edition, John Wiley & Sons, 2003, pp. 307-17.

[9] Pension Protection Act of 2006. A donor advised fund (DAF) was first defined in this legislation.

[10] Sklar v. Commissioner, 125 T.C. 14, 2005. The court rejected the claim that parents could deduct payments to a religious school on the basis that 55 percent of the cost of tuition related to religious instruction. The court concluded, "Not only has the Supreme Court held that, generally, a payment for which one receives consideration does not constitute a contribution or gift ... but it has explicitly rejected the contention ... that there is an exception for payments for which one receives only religious benefits in return."

[11] Statement of Financial Accounting Standards 116, par. 14, June 1993.

[12] *Ibid.*

[13] Revenue Ruling 79-249. While seeking contributions to pay for a portion of the cost of constructing a multi-purpose building, a municipal board of education told donors that all contributions would be refunded if sufficient funds were not raised and that any excess donations would be retained by the board for general school purposes. The contributions were not deductible as charitable contributions until they were transferred to the construction fund or retained for general school purposes.

[14] Also, Comment to ¶413 of The Uniform Trust Code, promulgated by the National Conference of Commissioners on Uniform State Laws (NCCUSL) in 2000 and amended in 2001, 2003 and 2005, which provides in part: "if a particular charitable purpose becomes unlawful, impracticable, impossible to achieve, or wasteful ... the court may apply *cy pres* to modify or terminate the trust ... in a manner consistent with the settlor's charitable purposes." UPMIFA, as adopted July 2006, Comment to Section 6, similarly allows a release of restrictions with donor permission, and permits deviations to modify or release a restriction, through court order or upon notification to the State Attorney General (or other applicable charity official). Modifications from the original intent of the donor must be "in accordance with the donor's probable intention" for deviation, and "in a manner consistent with the charitable purposes expressed in the gift instrument" for *cy pres.*

[15] Restatement (Third) of Trusts (2003), par. 67.

Also, Fremont-Smith, Marion R., *Governing Nonprofit Organizations: Federal and State Law and Regulations,* The Belknap Press of Harvard University Press, pp. 173-86, provides a thorough discussion of the application of the *cy pres* doctrine.

[16] Restatement (Third) of Trusts, supra note 125, par. 66.

[17] Revenue Ruling 76-150. Under the "tax benefit rule," a contribution that is refunded in a subsequent year may generate taxable income in the year of the refund, if it generated a tax deduction in the year of contribution.

[18] Treasury Regulation 1.170A-9(e)(11)(V)(B), (C) and (D)

[19] Edie, John A., "Use of Fiscal Agents: A Trap for the Unwary," Council on Foundations, 1989.

[20] Toce, et. al., *Tax Economics of Charitable Giving,* 2005/2006 Edition, Warren, Gorham & Lamont of RIA, 2005, pp. 4-18.

[21] Huetter and Brockner, "Conduit Organizations — Charitable Deductibility and Exemption Issues," Continuing Professional Education, Exempt Organizations Technical Instruction Program for FY 1995, Department of the Treasury.

[22] Tripp v. Commissioner, 337 F.2d 432 (7th Cir. 1964). A taxpayer made a contribution to a college and identified the individual student whom he wished to benefit from the funds. The taxpayer stated, "I am aware that a donation to a Scholarship Fund is only deductible if it is unspecified, however, if in your opinion and that of the authorities, it could be applied to the advantage of Mr. Robert F. Roble, I think it would be constructive." The court held that the intent to benefit a particular person precluded a contribution deduction, even though the person was unrelated to the taxpayer, and the person might have been an appropriate scholarship recipient had the college used its own funds. The Tax Court ruled that the gift was not deductible.

Also, Thomason, 2 T.C. 441 (1943). Payments to a charitable organization to reimburse it for the expenses of maintaining a particular child were not deductible because the organization did not have the exclusive right of appropriation of the funds donated, but had to use them only for the designated child.

Also, Revenue Ruling 61-66. No charitable deduction was permitted for a transfer of money to a university to enable a specified teacher to engage in research. The university had no control over the disposition of the funds; it acted merely as a conduit.

[23] Dan Busby, "Running Gifts 'Through' the Ministry," FOCUS on Accountability, ECFA, Third Quarter 2005

[24] Internal Revenue Code 170(f)(10), personal benefit contract provisions added by the Tax Relief Extension Act of 1999

[25] Revenue Ruling 69-573. If a contribution is to a qualified donee but earmarked for a nonqualified donee—including for an individual—the contribution is to the nonqualified donee and is not deductible.

[26] Davis v. U.S., 495 U.S. 472 (1990). Mr. and Mrs. Davis claimed charitable deductions for funds transferred to their sons while they were serving as full-time, unpaid missionaries for the Church of Jesus Christ of Latter-day Saints (the Church). The Church requested the payments, set their amounts, and, through written guidelines, instructed that they be used exclusively for missionary work. The court held that the payments were not "for the use of" the Church because the Church lacked sufficient possession and control of the funds.

[27] Charleston Chair Co. v. U.S., 203 F.Supp. 126 (E.D.S.C. 1962). A corporation was denied a deduction for amounts given to a foundation established to provide educational opportunities for employees and their children. The court noted that the narrow class of persons who might benefit, the more restricted group that did benefit and the preference given to the son of the director, stockholder and trustee disclosed that the foundation was not operated exclusively for charitable purposes.

[28] Russell v. Allen, 107 U.S. 163. The beneficiary of a charitable contribution must be indefinite.

[29] Private Letter Ruling 200530016. Although the ruling does not convey a new position by the IRS, it is an excellent summary. It emphasizes the importance of the donee's control and discretion as to the use of a donation. It also highlights that gifts are earmarked by the donor for a particular individual, and the donee organization exercises no control or discretion over their use, the gifts are not deductible as charitable contributions.

[30] Internal Revenue Code 170(c).

[31] Rockefeller v. Commissioner, 676 F.2d 35, 40 (2d Cir. 1982). Legislative history of the law that added the phrase "to or for the use of" in defining a contribution.

Also, Bruce R. Hopkins, *The Tax Law of Charitable Giving,* Third Edition, 2005, John Wiley & Sons, pp. 370-71.

[32] There are many cases illustrating this point. See Tripp ([22]) and Thomason ([22]).

[33] Internal Revenue Code 4958. This section of the Code relates to intermediate sanctions—the imposition of an excise tax on disqualified persons (insiders) receiving an excess benefit from the organization. An excess benefit is an economic benefit provided in excess of the value of the consideration received.

[34] Claudia L. Kelley and Douglas Roberts, "Reconciling Church Benevolence and the Tax Law," Taxation for Exempts, September/October, 2006.

[35] IRS Publication 1828, "Disaster Relief," revised September 2005, pp. 18-19.

[36] Revenue Ruling 2003-12. This ruling states that "a payment made to an individual by a charity that responds to the individual's needs, and does not proceed from any moral or legal duty, is motivated by detached and disinterested generosity" is a tax-free gift and, therefore, does not trigger Form 1099-MISC filing requirements.

[37] Winters v. Commissioner, 468 F.2d 778 (2nd Cir. 1972). The taxpayer and the charity attempted to eliminate the quid pro quo nature of the transaction. The school did not officially charge "tuition." Contributions were requested but not compelled and the schools represented that no student would be turned away for failure to contribute to the school. Nevertheless, because the taxpayers expected, and in fact received, a valuable benefit in the form of religious-oriented education for their children, the court recognized that the taxpayers' "voluntary" contributions were, in effect, payments of tuition.

Also, Sklar v. Commissioner([10])

Also, Tripp ([22]) and Revenue Ruling 79-81. "Sponsors" paid the tuition for students at a school. The sponsor was often the student's parent. The IRS denied a charitable contribution deduction because of indications that the payments were designated for the benefit of particular students.

[38] Revenue Ruling 83-104. The charitable deduction was dependent on "whether a reasonable person, taking all the facts and circumstances of the case in due account, would conclude that enrollment in the school was in no manner contingent upon making the payment, that the payment was not made pursuant to a plan (whether express or implied) to convert nondeductible tuition into charitable contributions, and that receipt of the benefit was not otherwise dependent upon the making of the payment."

[39] Private Letter Ruling 9338014. A charitable deduction is allowed when a committee has the power to select recipients based on criteria emphasizing needs, even though the donor's relatives could be recipients of aid from a scholarship fund established by the donor. The IRS stressed that no understanding existed for the donor's relatives to be preferred in the selection process.

[40] Revenue Procedure 76-47. This Revenue Procedure outlines the requirements when scholarships for employee dependents may be considered nontaxable.

[41] INFO-2006-0027. In this Private Letter Ruling, the IRS ruled a charity that helps low-incomers pay for the cost of an adoption is exempt from 1099 reporting if the aid is given directly to the individuals. Additionally, the aid is treated as a nontaxable gift (Rev. Rul. 2003-12).

[42] Also, Thomason ([22]), Private Letter Ruling 200530016

[43] Revenue Ruling 63-252. In this ruling, the IRS analyzes five situations relating to contributions provided to foreign organizations. The examples are used to draw on the principles in case law that recognize that special earmarking of the use or destination of funds paid to a qualifying charitable organization may deprive the donor of a deduction.

[44] IRS Publication 526, Charitable Contributions, revised 2006, for limitations that apply to treaties with Canada, Mexico, and Israel. Contributions to foreign organizations located in these

countries may be an exception to the general rule that contributions to foreign organizations are not tax-deductible.

[45] Bruce R. Hopkins, *The Tax Law of Charitable Giving,* Third Edition, John Wiley & Sons, 2005, pp. 550-53

[46] John Butler, *Donor Advised Funds Side Affects,* Capin Crouse LLP, Email Alert, 2007

[47] Technical Advice Memorandum (TAM) 94-05-003. A student enrolled in a school's program of study leading to a Master of Divinity degree. As part of the degree requirements, students had to complete a program of practical education, which included field education and an internship. Each student received academic credit upon completion of the internship portion of the program. The school granted credit for the internship regardless of whether the student was compensated for the service.

Another nonprofit organization enabled seminary students to receive support for the ministries in which they serve. Seminary students become self-employed contractors with the second nonprofit. Their support comes from tax-deductible contributions by donors whom the seminary students contact. A donor usually gives a certain amount periodically for the ministry of a particular student. Contributions to the second nonprofit are earmarked for the student by use of account numbers and envelopes with the student's name. The donations are directed to the second nonprofit, which maintains a separate account for each student. The TAM found that the donors intended to benefit an individual, rather than the second nonprofit and held that the contributions were not "to" the charity, and therefore were not deductible as charitable contributions.

[48] Peace v. Commissioner, 43 T.C. 1(1964). A donor made contributions to Sudan Interior Mission (now SIM) and indicated on the check that the contributions were to be used for the support of four specific missionaries. The mission's policy was to pool all funds received for missionaries and equally divide the total received each month among all the missionaries. The donor was familiar with the policy of the mission to pool contributions. The mission had exclusive control, under its own policy, of both the administration and the distribution of the funds donated. The donor intended to benefit the mission and not the individual missionaries. The tax court found that the contributions were deductible.

For a contribution to be deductible when made to a qualified donee and accompanied by a suggestion that the contribution be spent to support an individual engaged in the donee's exempt activities, the donee must have complete discretion and control over the contribution and the donor must understand that the donee has such complete discretion and control and thus intend the contribution to the qualified donee.

[49] Great Commission Ministries (GCM) was denied tax-exempt status in 1996 over GCM's deputized fund-raising practices. In 1997, the IRS decided not to defend its position in court against GCM. The IRS exonerated GCM's policies and practices and issued GCM a tax-exemption determination letter.

[50] Letter from IRS, Exempt Organizations Division, May 26, 1999.

[51] Letter from IRS, Exempt Organizations Division, January, 2000.

[52] Copeland and Jones, "Deputized Fundraising," Continuing Professional Education Exempt Organizations Technical Instruction Program for FY 1999, Department of the Treasury.

Also, Shoemaker, et. al., "Donor Control," Exempt Organizations Continuing Professional Education Technical Instruction Program for FY 1999 (1998).

[53] See Peace ([48]), Tripp ([22])

Also, McMillian, 31 T.C. 1143 (1959). A charitable deduction was disallowed because the taxpayer's primary intent was not to benefit the adoption agency but was to satisfy his personal desire to adopt a child.

Also, Revenue Ruling 68-484. Amounts paid by a corporation under a program to provide financial support in the form of scholarships and grants-in-aid to exempt educational institutions are deductible as charitable contributions. Some of the scholarships were made available to institutions that had a certain number of graduates employed by the corporation and certain scholarships were made available to institutions from which the corporation drew a substantial number of graduates.

Also, Revenue Ruling 79-81. The IRS concluded that contributions solicited by members of a religious organization for participation in a leadership training program were not deductible because the facts evidenced the contributor's intent to benefit the individual recipient and the organization did not have control over the donated funds.

Also, General Counsel Memorandum 32045 (July 27, 1961). The "intended benefit test" was employed when a fund collected contributions from fraternity alumni to assist one of the fraternity's chapters construct a new fraternity house. The fund turned the contributions over to the university. The university agreed to lend them with interest to the fraternity chapter in return for a second mortgage on the building to be constructed. The university would be entitled to use the interest to award scholarships to students of its choice. While recognizing that benefits would accrue to the university under the proposed arrangement, the IRS nevertheless held that the university was "merely a conduit for the cash contributions to and for the benefit of the fraternity," and that the contributions to the proposed fund would not be deductible as gifts or contributions to or for the use of the university.

[54] Revenue Ruling 68-67. Voluntary contributions made directly to and for the support of employee-missionaries performing services to further the purposes and objectives of a mission were deemed paid on behalf of the mission and in consideration for services rendered by the missionaries and were includible in the gross income of the missionaries. At issue were the gifts given directly to the missionaries by individuals or groups. The IRS determined the gifts in question were includible in the missionary's gross income.

Also, Winn v. Commissioner, 595 F.2d 1060 (5th Cir. 1979). At issue was a contribution in response to an appeal by a church to assist a certain person in her church missionary work. Central to the court's finding was that even though the contribution was made payable to a fund named for the individual, an officer of the church took the funds donated and dealt with them as the church wished. Possession of the contribution by a church official was held to be one of the elements establishing control by the donee.

[55] See letter from IRS ([50]).

[56] Greene v. Commissioner, T.C. Memo 1996-531. Richard G. and Anne C. Greene petitioned the U.S. tax court asking the court to

overturn a determination made by the IRS that Rev. Greene was an employee of the Department of Foreign Mission (DFM), General Counsel of the Assemblies of God.

Rev. Greene took the position that the General Counsel of the Assemblies of God did not exert the degree of control that would normally exist in an employer-employee relationship. DFM did not invest in Rev. Greene's work facilities, provided Rev. Greene with no employee benefits, and did not have the right to terminate Rev. Greene as a missionary. While both the DFM and Rev. Greene hoped for a permanent relationship, Rev. Greene was free to resign his position at any time. Both parties operated under the belief that Rev. Greene was self-employed.

The court ruled that Rev. Greene was self-employed for income tax purposes.

[57] Internal Revenue Code 132, Regulation 1.61-21

[58] Revenue Ruling 79-81

[59] Internal Revenue Code 409A, entitled "Inclusion in Gross Income of Deferred Compensation under Nonqualified Deferred Compensation Plans," was added to the Code in October 2004 as part of the American Jobs Creation Act of 2004. The final regulations were issued on April 10, 2007.

[60] Internal Revenue Code 170(j)

[61] Internal Revenue Service Publication 526, Charitable Contributions, revised 2006

[62] See Davis ([26])

[63] Richard F. Larkin, "Give Your Financial Statement a Check-up," FOCUS on Accountability, ECFA, First Quarter 2006

[64] AICPA *Not-for-Profit Audit Guide,* par. 5.42, May 2007

[65] Statement on Financial Accounting Standards 116, par. 16

[66] AICPA *Not-for-Profit Audit Guide,* par. 5.45, May 2007

[67] AICPA *Not-for-Profit Audit Guide,* par. 5.40, May 2007

[68] AICPA *Not-for-Profit Audit Guide,* par. 3.27 and 10.13, May 2007

[69] T. Boone Pickens gift, as reported in the New York Times: Late in 2005, Mr. Pickens contributed $165 million to O.S.U. Cowboy Golf, a tiny charity that benefits the Oklahoma State University golf team. The New York Times reports that within an hour of receiving the gift, the charity invested the entire $165 million in BP Capital Management, a hedge fund controlled by Mr. Pickens. Pickens is also on the nine-member board of the charity.

Also, Barbara Bush gift, as reported by The Associated Press: In March 2006, Mrs. Bush, the former First Lady, made a contribution of an undisclosed amount to a Hurricane Katrina relief fund, conditioned on the use of the money to purchase educational software from Ignite Learning, a company founded and run by her son, Neil.

Also, Alan F. Rothschild, Jr., "How Donors May—and May Not—Exercise Control of Charitable Gifts," Taxation of Exempts, November/December 2004.

[70] Internal Revenue Code 6115(a). The 1993 Tax Act codified the requirement for charities to communicate to and educate donors about the deductibility (or lack thereof) of payments made to charities.

Also, *Tax Economics of Charitable Giving,* Toce, et. al., Warren, Gorham & Lamont, 2005, pp. 9-24 – 9-31.

Also, Wilkinson, et. al., *Charitable Giving Answer Book,* 2006 Edition, CCH, 2005, pp. 2-4, 5.

[71] *A Desktop Guide for Nonprofit Directors, Officers and Advisors,* Jack B. Siegel, John Wiley & Sons, 2006, pp. 450-52

[72] IRS Publication 3833, Disaster Relief, revised September 2005

[73] *Accounting and Reporting Guide for Christian Ministries,* Evangelical Joint Accounting Committee, 2001 (www.ecfa.org)

Also, Dan Busby, *Church and Nonprofit Tax & Financial Guide,* 2008 Edition, 2007, Zondervan

Also, Gross, et. al., *Financial and Accounting Guide for Not-for-Profit Organizations,* Seventh Edition, John Wiley & Sons, 2005, pp. 282-83

Glossary of Terms

Board-designated net assets – Unrestricted net assets subject to self-imposed limits by action of the governing board, *e.g.*, future programs, investment, contingencies, purchases, or construction of fixed assets, or other uses.

Capital campaign – Capital campaigns are used to raise funds for buildings, endowments, scholarships and other purposes. They generally include a quiet phase focusing on lead gifts (see "Lead Gifts"), an intermediate phase focusing on major gifts from the philanthropic community, and a public phase encouraging generous and modest gifts from a broad base of supporters.

Conduit gift – A nondeductible transfer of funds to a charity that is not intended to benefit the charity, and over which the charity does not have adequate discretion and control. Also, a transfer that has *not* been made to a charity in a deductible form because the recipient charity's function is as an agent for a particular noncharitable recipient. Also called a pass-through or earmarked gift.

Contribution – An unconditional transfer of cash or other assets to an entity or a settlement of cancellation of its liabilities in a voluntary nonreciprocal transfer by another entity acting other than as an owner.

Deputized fund-raising – Charities using this concept generally determine an amount each staff member is responsible to raise. Funds are often recorded in a support account for each worker. Charges are made against the support account that funds the staff member's particular sphere of the organization's ministry

Designated net assets – See board-designated net assets.

Documentation of disaster relief payments – Adequate records should demonstrate the victims' needs for the assistance provided, including:

- a complete description of the assistance;
- the purpose for which the aid was given;
- the charity's objective for disbursing assistance under each program;

- how the recipients were selected;
- the name, address, and amount distributed to each recipient, and
- any relationship between a recipient and officers, directors, or key employees or of substantial contributions to the charity.

Donor advised fund – A donor advised fund is a fund or account (1) separately identified by reference to contributions of a donor or donors, (2) owned and controlled by a sponsoring organization, and (3) as to which a donor (or any person appointed or designated by the donor) has, or reasonably expects to have, advisory privileges as to the distribution or investment of amounts held in the fund or account by reason of the donor's status as a donor.

Donor-imposed condition – A donor stipulation that specifies a future and uncertain event whose occurrence or failure to occur gives the promisor a right-of-return of assets he or she has transferred, or releases the promisor from its obligation to transfer assets.

Donor-imposed restriction – A donor stipulation that specifies a use for the contributed asset that is more specific than the broad limits imposed by the charity's purpose and nature. This may result from the nature of the organization, the environment in which it operates, and the purposes specified in its articles of incorporation or bylaws, or comparable documents for an unincorporated association. A restriction on an organization's use of the contributed asset may be temporary or permanent.

Earmarked gift – See conduit gift.

Explicit gift restriction – An explicit gift restriction occurs when a donor sends a letter, indicates a restriction on a response form, or provides other specific communication to the charity identifying a contribution as restricted in terms of purpose or time.

Fiscal agent – One who acts for or in place of another based on limited financial or accounting authority from the person engaging the agent. The term "fiscal agent" has no specific legal meaning. The term is not found in the exempt organization sections of the Internal Revenue Code.

There is a misperception that when grants or gifts cannot be made directly, all one must do is transfer the money through a convenient "fiscal agent," which is frequently a well-established public charity. While there are proper ways to use intermediary organizations with respect to a charitable gift, too often the term "fiscal agent" has the negative connotation of a "laundering agent."

Implicit gift restriction – An implicit gift restriction occurs when there are certain circumstances surrounding the gift that makes the donor's restriction clear even though there is no explicit gift restriction.

Lead gifts – The first, usually sizable, gifts of a capital campaign. The gifts are often given by someone loyal to an organization's mission who wants to help kick off a capital campaign and/or to entice others to participate in contributing as well.

National worker (non-U.S. worker) – A citizen, born in or naturalized in the country where an organization conducts missionary activity. A co-laborer and partner who desires that the Gospel be preached and the evangelical church in his or her country be established and grow to point of reproduction. The service of national workers may either be as an employee (hired) or as a missionary (primarily supported locally). A national worker does not need a visa to enter or work in his or her home country.

Needy and distressed test – This test should include a set of criteria by which a charity can objectively make distributions to individuals who are financially or otherwise distressed. Adequate records should support the basis upon which assistance is provided.

Permanently-restricted gift – A gift restricted in perpetuity by the donor. Contributions from a donor who has stipulated that the principal remain intact in perpetuity are also referred to as "pure" or "true" endowments.

Permanently-restricted net assets – The part of net assets for a nonprofit organization that is restricted in perpetuity by donor-imposed stipulations.

Personal gifts – A transfer of money or other property from one individual to another individual, voluntarily, without any obligation nor a consideration for services rendered.

Pooled fund-raising – Funds raised to support a group of workers instead of a particular worker. There might be just one group—all the self-supported workers in one mission field. Or, the group might be a team of workers in several mission fields.

Preferenced gift – A preference indicated by a donor expressing the donor's wishes, desires, or advice on how or when the gift will be used but is not restricted for a specific individual. Preferenced gifts are generally recorded as temporarily restricted because the gifts are restricted for a certain purpose and the preference relates to greater specificity than the organization's overall purpose.

Quid pro quo – When a donor receives goods or services of value approximate to the amount transferred, there is no true gift. This is because the person received something in exchange for the transfer, and thus, there is a transaction that is a purchase rather than a gift.

Reclassifications of net assets – These are the simultaneous increases in one net asset class and decreases in another that are made if (a) the organization fulfills the purposes for which the net assets were restricted, (b) donor-imposed restrictions expire with the passage of time or with the death of a split interest agreement beneficiary (if the net assets are not otherwise restricted), (c) a donor withdraws, or court action removes, previously imposed restrictions, or (d) donors impose restrictions on otherwise unrestricted net assets. For example, the amount of a donor's contribution that must be used by the organization for a specified program would be reclassified from temporarily restricted to unrestricted net assets in the period in which the organization conducts the program.

Restatement of prior-period financial statements – Any error in the financial statements of a prior period discovered subsequent to their issuance should be reported as a prior-period adjustment by restating the prior-period financial statements. Restatements of prior-period financial statements are sometimes confused with the reclassifications of net assets (see the above definition of reclassifications of net assets).

Restricted net assets – Resources whose use is restricted by an outside agency or person, as contrasted with those that the charity may use for any activity within its exempt purpose(s).

Restriction – A donor stipulation that limits the time or purpose of a gift's use. The purpose limitation must be more specific than the broad limits imposed by the charity's purpose or nature.

Short-term mission trips – A domestic or international trip sponsored by a church or other charity for a duration of a few days to two years. Trip participants sometimes only involve adults. Other times, participants are minors, supervised by adults, or some combination of adults and minors.

Stipulation – A statement by a donor which creates a condition or restriction on the use of the transferred resources.

Temporarily-restricted gift – A gift that is donor restricted for a stated period of time or until a stated event has occurred. The stated event must be more specific than the broad limits imposed by the charity's purpose or nature. If the stated period of time or stated event has not occurred, a temporarily-restricted gift is reflected as a temporarily-restricted net asset on the charity's statement of financial position.

Temporarily-restricted net assets – The part of net assets for a nonprofit organization that is temporarily restricted by donor-imposed stipulations.

Underwater funds – A fund in which the principal amount (corpus) has fallen below the value of when originally gifted by the donor. This is usually the result of investment and market contractions.

Underwater funds rule – Under UMIFA, an organization was prohibited from using fund assets if the value of the fund was below its historic dollar value. UPMIFA removes this restriction and gives the trustees discretion to make this decision in accordance with internal policies governing those trustees.

Unrestricted net assets – Resources that have no external restriction on use or purpose. These can be used for any purpose designated by the governing board within the organization's exempt purpose or nature, as distinguished from resources restricted externally for specific purposes.

Variance power – A variance power is the authority granted to a charity by a court with respect to the use of a donor-restricted gift. The term may also be used regarding the authority a charity believes it has over a donor-restricted gift because of disclaimers or caveats communicated to donors relating to the use of gifts when under- or over-funding of a project or campaign occurs.

Index

ECFA Standards Relating to Donor-Restricted Gifts

Standard 4 – Use of Resources – Every member shall exercise the management and financial controls necessary to provide reasonable assurance that all resources are used (nationally and internationally) in conformity with applicable federal and state laws and regulations to accomplish the exempt purposes for which they are intended.

Standard 5 – Financial Disclosure – Every member shall provide a copy of its current financial statements upon written request and provide other disclosures as the law may require. If audited financial statements are required to comply with Standard 3, they must be disclosed under this Standard. An organization must provide a report, on written request, including financial information, on any specific project for which it is soliciting gifts.

Standard 7.2 – Communication and Donor Expectations: Fund-raising appeals must not create unrealistic donor expectations of what a donor's gift will actually accomplish within the limits of the organization's ministry.

Standard 7.3 – Communication and Donor Intent: All statements made by the organization in its fund-raising appeals about the use of the gift must be honored by the organization. The donor's intent is related both to what was communicated in the appeal and to any donor instructions accompanying the gift. The organization should be aware that communications made in fund-raising appeals may create a legally binding restriction.

Standard 7.6 – Financial Advice: The representative of the organization, when dealing with persons regarding commitments on major estate assets, must seek to guide and advise donors so they have adequately considered the broad interests of the family and the various ministries they are currently supporting before they make final decisions. Donors should be encouraged to use the services of their attorneys, accountants, or other professional advisors.

Standard 7.8 – Tax-deductible Gifts for a Named Recipient's Personal Benefit: Tax-deductible gifts may not be used to pass money or benefits to any named individual for personal use.

Standard 7.10 – Acknowledgment of Gifts-in-Kind: Property or gifts-in-kind received by an organization should be acknowledged describing the property or gift accurately without a statement of the gift's market value. It is the responsibility of the donor to determine the fair market value of the property for tax purposes. The organization may be required to provide additional information for gifts of motor vehicles, boats, and airplanes.

Standard 7.11 – Acting in the Interest of the Donor: An organization must make every effort to avoid accepting a gift from or entering into a contract with a prospective donor which would knowingly place a hardship on the donor or place the donor's future well-being in jeopardy.

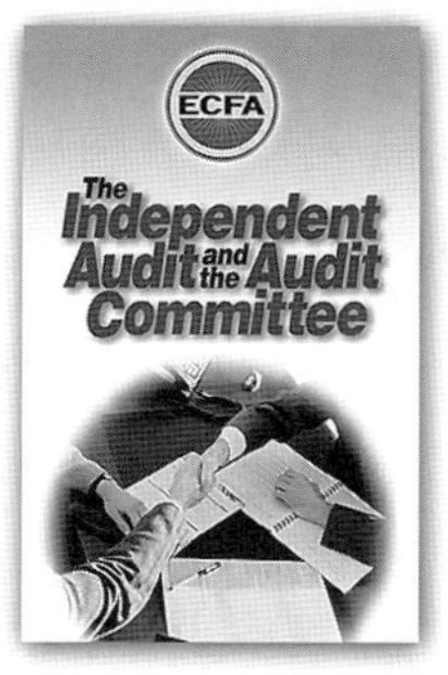

The Independent Audit and the Audit Committee

This 16-page booklet includes a wealth of information about obtaining a quality audit, selection and rotation of auditors or audit partners, auditor independence, the cost of an audit, branch and field auditing, the audit committee function, and includes a sample audit committee charter.

ECFA Standards and Best Practices

ECFA Standards and Best Practices for Churches

In addition to the Standards, ECFA has developed a series of best practices—including a set of best practices specifically for churches—to encourage member organizations to strive for the highest levels of excellence.

Order at: www.ECFA.org
or call 800-323-9473

Allocating and Reporting Ministry Expenses

This 24-page booklet includes a wealth of material explaining the accounting rules for functional expense allocation: management and general, allocating expenses between programs, fund-raising, and membership development. Financial statement examples and an excerpt from Form 990 are included.

Giving from the Heart

Designed for ministries to give to donors with or without an imprint. Both inspirational and motivational, this 32-page pocket-sized guide will help Christians make wise choices and find new ways to practice faithful stewardship. It is up-to-date with current charitable giving laws.

Custom imprinting available on the inside front or back cover.

Order at: www.ECFA.org
or call 800-323-9473